THE LEGEND OF CUSHETUNK

THE NATHAN SKINNER MANUSCRIPT AND THE EARLY HISTORY OF COCHECTON

Barbara J. Sivertsen
and *Barbara L. Covey*

HERITAGE BOOKS
2011

HERITAGE BOOKS

AN IMPRINT OF HERITAGE BOOKS, INC.

Books, CDs, and more—Worldwide

For our listing of thousands of titles see our website
at
www.HeritageBooks.com

Published 2011 by
HERITAGE BOOKS, INC.
Publishing Division
100 Railroad Ave. #104
Westminster, Maryland 21157

Other Heritage Books by the authors:

Rebecca Kellogg Ashley, 1695–1757: From Deerfield to Onaquaga
Barbara L. Covey

Turtles, Wolves, and Bears: A Mohawk Family History
Barbara J. Sivertsen

International Standard Book Numbers
Paperbound: 978-1-55613-787-7
Clothbound: 978-0-7884-8888-7

TABLE OF CONTENTS

THE LEGEND OF CUSHETUNK

The early history of the Upper Delaware was invented, almost entirely, by a man named Nathan Skinner.

His version of what happened there during the American Revolution, and for the roughly twenty-one pioneer years preceding the war, has been quoted, usually verbatim, in at least three major local histories of the region.

By "Upper Delaware" we mean the long valley paralleling the river between Port Jervis, New York, on the south and Hancock, New York, on the north. Cushetunk was the Indian name given to this valley for about five miles on either side of today's Cochecton, New York. "Cushytunk" appears on one of the earliest maps of the region, done by Lewis Evans in 1749. In later maps, Evans gave the name to the range of mountains there, on the Pennsylvania side.

When James Eldridge Quinlan, a junior editor for *The Republican Watchman* in Monticello, New York, began writing a series of columns on the local history of the area in 1850, he turned to a seventy-three-year old man living in Cochecton, New York--Nathan Skinner. Skinner had grown up in Cushetunk, learning the local history second-hand from the survivors of the French and Indian War and the Revolution. He had already written down some of these tales, and had a collection of early deeds handed down to him from his father.

We do not know if the whole or a part of the Nathan Skinner Manuscript had been written when Quinlan first began writing about the area, but by 1873, when he came to write his *History of Sullivan County*, Quinlan used copies of the manuscript and deeds given to him by Nathan Skinner. In most cases, Quinlan's version of the Cushetunk story does not depart from Skinner's.

The same thing happened in 1880, when Phineas G. Goodrich published his *History of Wayne County, Pennsylvania*, and a third time with Alfred Matthews' *History of Wayne, Pike, and Monroe Counties, Pennsylvania* in 1886. Both books quote large portions of the manuscript.

Copies of the manuscript, in Nathan Skinner's exceedingly small handwriting, passed to his descendants. One of these copies reached the hands of the Reverend Charles Nelson Sinnett, an itinerant Presbyterian and Congregational pastor in North Dakota and Minnesota. Sinnett, the author of histories of many New England families, copied, arranged, and indexed the manuscript, now called *Pioneer Days at Cochecton, New York*, in 1924 and distributed his work to various libraries, including the Grosvenor Library in Buffalo, New York, and the Newberry Library in Chicago, Illinois.

Many years later, in 1951, Doris Seymour Wahl of Niagara Falls, New York, discovered Sinnett's copy of the manuscript in the Grosvenor Library. For two years she painstakingly copied the manuscript by hand. Then she sent it for comparison to Mrs. Edna Skinner Beegle, who had an original handwritten copy. Mrs. Wahl published her copy in *The Skinner Kinsmen*. It was reprinted by Arthur N. Meyers in *The Sullivan County Democrat* and later by him as a pamphlet in 1970.

Like our predecessors, we, the authors of *THE LEGEND OF CUSHETUNK: THE NATHAN SKINNER MANUSCRIPT AND THE EARLY HISTORY OF COCHECTON*, came to the Nathan Skinner Manuscript eager and anxious to find an authoritative voice to tell us what really happened in Cushetunk and Cochecton during the early years.

One of us is working on a fictional account of the life of William Tegawirunte, half-breed son of Sir William Johnson, colonial superintendent of Indian affairs, whose adventures during the Revolution carried him into the Cushetunk region.

The other has ancestors who lived at Cushetunk during the pioneer period and early days of the Revolution. They received short shrift from Nathan Skinner in his manuscript.

We were not the first to note that Skinner's manuscript probably was made up of a number of stories written over a period of years and either gathered together by him before his death (on November 15, 1856), or post mortem by his relatives. One of us, who has a computer, decided to rearrange the manuscript in chronological order, using the Sinnett typescript. We were both delighted to discover that things which did not make sense, earlier, now did have a logical sequence, and we thought it worth publishing this new, clearer version of the Nathan Skinner Manuscript.

But the new arrangement pointed out, even more strikingly, inconsistencies and errors of logic. For example, the one working on Tegawirunte's life knew that a local Loyalist sympathizer named Barney Kane had served under Joseph Brant, the Mohawk war chief, during the Revolution. Nathan Skinner's version, repeated in the local histories, states that Kane's family had been killed by Mohawks. This made no sense.

We also noticed omissions and evasions. We had learned from the Public Papers of New York Governor George Clinton that Cochecton (ergo Cushetunk) played a key role in the Revolutionary War, since it was the sole connection, overland, between the British at Niagara and those in New York after the city had been taken by the British in July, 1776. No hint of Cushetunk's importance as a Tory stronghold appears in the Nathan Skinner Manuscript. Another case is a particularly convoluted paragraph on William Tryon's assumption of the office of royal governor of New York colony in 1771. These and other parts of the manuscript are probably Nathan Skinner's attempt to gloss over his family's Loyalist sympathies.

It became obvious that we needed to add contemporary factual materials to support, challenge, and enhance the manuscript. Our sources were the archives of Pennsylvania and New York, the published papers of Sir William Johnson, George Clinton, and the Susquehannah Company, the unpublished Draper and Haldimand manuscripts, and many others.

We learned a great deal about pioneer times and the Revolutionary period in Cochecton/Cushetunk and we invite readers interested in this time and place to follow us where our historical journey has led. We have not set out to challenge dearly-held traditions in the valley, based on the Nathan Skinner Manuscript or on other early histories. We see our efforts as supplementing the stories in the manuscript, and putting them into historical focus. We would like to thank Nathan Skinner for writing down what he had heard, since apparently few others in the valley thought it important to preserve their past. Without the Skinner Manuscript we would know very little about the personal and human side of the early days at Cushetunk.

MAP OF COCHECTON-CUSHETUNK

The map is based upon: (1) the U.S. Geological Survey's 7.5 minute topographic maps of Callicoon and Damascus; (2) the *Atlas of Sullivan County* (F. W. Beers, editor, Walker and Jewett Publisher, New York, 1875; (3) the *Atlas of Wayne County* (F. W. Beers, editor, A. Pomeroy & Co., New York, 1872); (4) *Upper Delaware Magazine, Summer 1978* (Catskill-Delaware Publications, Inc.) p. 34-35; (5) National Park Service's *Cultural Resources Survey*, Volumes 1 and 5 (1982); (6) letters in Draper's Brant Papers, 17F; and (7) the descriptions given in the Skinner Manuscript and following Notes.

The first page of the map shows the northern half of Cochecton, the second page, the southern half. The broken lines mark the extent of the flat lands next to the river as indicated in the Geological Survey's maps. The numbers on the map refer to the following locations (page numbers refer to the Skinner Manuscript):

1 **Hollister place or Widow Hollister place**. It was here that Daniel Skinner built his mill shortly before the Revolution (pages 21, 28).

2 **Dremor's Island** (pages 8, 28).

3 **Grant's place** (pages 8, 28).

4 **Joseph Ross place, brook, and eddy** (pages 8, 9). It is possible that Ross's house was slightly farther south within the small spit of land that juts out into the river.

5 **Nat Evans house** (page 13). This is the 1872 residence of Moses Tyler in the Wayne County Atlas.

6 **Daniel Skinner house** (page 13). This is the 1872 residence of a G. Bush in the Wayne County Atlas.

7 **David Young place** (page 9 and note 29)

8 **William Conklin's place** (page 9).

9 **Cadoshe's place** (page 9). This is approximate. Cadoshe was also said to have had a farm by "the creek that bears his name," a mile north of Hancock, N.Y., at the time of the Revolution (Draper 17F101a).

10 **Bezaleel Tyler I and Paul Tyler's place** (page 6). This is approximate.

11 **Lemuel Burcham place** (pages 9).

12 **Nathan Parks' place** (page 8). This is an approximate location based on the location of Parks Brook.

13 **Bezaleel Tyler II and George Bush place** (page 10). See also the 1872 Wayne County map.

14 **Old Fort** (pages 0, 29). This was the blockhouse on the New York side, below Cochecton Bridge. The location is approximate.

15 **Nicholas Conklin place** (page 29). Skinner's description is incomplete, but this is the approximate location. Mary Curtis, Cultural Resources Specialist for the National Park Service, Narrowsburg, N.Y., says that Nicholas Conklin also had a place on the Pennsylvania side near the Baptist Church (letter from Patricia Christian, June 2, 1992).

16 **Nathan Mitchell place** (page 29). Nathan Mitchell may have lived on the north side of the creek which bears his name.

17 **Moses Thomas blockhouse** (page 8). There is one dry stone wall and remains of the well remaining of the blockhouse, which in 1970 was on the property of James Card.

18 **John Land house** (page 28 and note 58).

19 **Aaron Thomas and Robert Land house** (see notes 58 and 13).

20 **Bryant Kane place** (page 29). The Skinner description is specific to this location.

21 **John Lassely place** (page 28). This is an approximate location on the flats south of Milanville. Soloman Decker's place would have been south of here, off the map. Aaron Thomas settled near here (see note 58).

ACKNOWLEDGMENT

We gratefully acknowledge the help from Patricia Christian of the Equinunk Historical Society in providing a great many useful maps and other material and for her painstaking efforts to achieve the accuracy of these maps.

Nonetheless, we have made the final decisions on the placement of map locations ourselves, and we take complete responsibility for them and whatever errors they might contain.

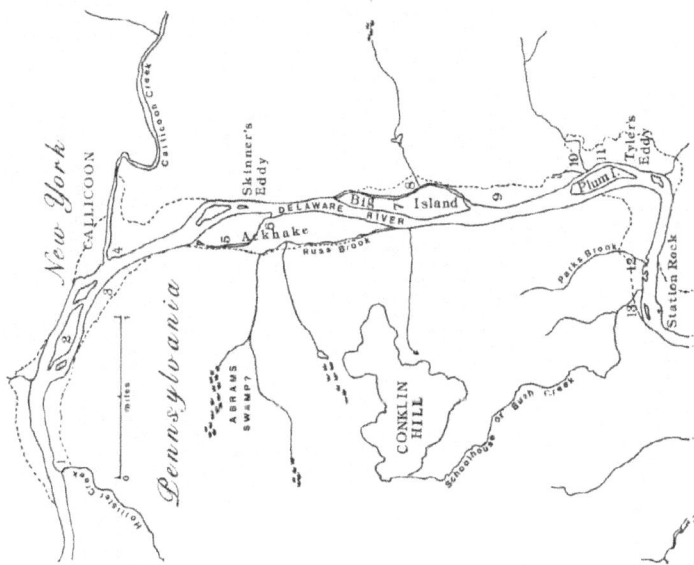

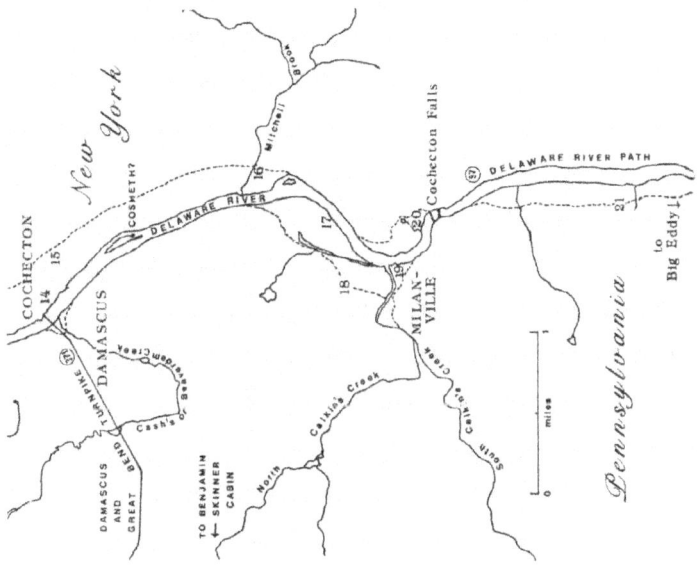

New York

COCHECTON
14 15
COSMETH?
DELAWARE RIVER
DAMASCUS
Cash's Creek
TURNPIKE 13

DAMASCUS
AND
GREAT
BEND

TO BENJAMIN
SKINNER
CABIN

Blue Creek
Mitchell
16
17
18

North
Catkin's Creek
Catkin's Creek

MILAN-
VILLE

North Calkin's Creek
South Calkin's Creek

Cochecton Falls
20
37 DELAWARE RIVER PATH
21

to
Big Eddy

Pennsylvania

0   1
miles

THE NATHAN SKINNER MANUSCRIPT
AND THE EARLY HISTORY OF COCHECTON

Cochecton and Cushetunk

Cochecton, New York, in 1783 commenced about a mile below Cochecton Falls (or at Horse's Island) and ran in the river at Hollister's Creek, about one and a half miles above Callicoon, a distance of about twelve miles in length and not exceeding a half mile in breadth. It was wilderness from there: mountains to the eastward at least thirty miles, and westward to the Susquehanna. The name of the settlement originated from Cosheth and Cushetunk, both Indian names. Cosheth was a small point of land projecting from the east bank of the river about a mile below Cochecton bridge, making a small cove below it, which made a convenient landing place for a canoe. The vicinity of Calkin's Creek and Cochecton Falls was called Cushetunk. The definition of the first word is "made land," and of the latter, "foaming water."[1]

There was a scattering of places above and below Cochecton, which were always inquired for by their appropriate names. The first below was called Utter's Eddy, and others called it Halbert's. It afterwards became known as Haman's, and now is known as Big Eddy. The first place above Cochecton was called Island and then Rock Run, Pine Flat, Little Equinunk, Old Basket, Long Eddy, Big Equinunk, Equinunk Island, Topetoke, and Shehawken.

There was an old Indian path through the woods on which no carriage could travel. Nevertheless there were many who made their way into this country by the strength of feet and legs, or by the power of hands and arms which they used in pushing themselves up the river in a canoe, or by swinging their feet one before the other.

On July 11, 1754, twelve hundred Yankees, under the sanction of the Connecticut Colony, obtained a deed for a tract of land extending from the Susquehanna to the Delaware River. It was signed by eighteen of the principal chiefs of the Six Nations.[2] Chapman says in his *History of Wyoming*

1

that in the summer of 1757 the Delaware (or Connecticut) Company commenced the settlement of Cushetunk, and that in 1760 the settlement contained thirty dwelling houses, three log houses, a grist mill, saw mill, and a block house.[3] The Connecticut Company laid out a town, made arrangements for the settlement, selected a place for the Meeting House, and surveyed a lot for a preacher. The center of this town was near where John Barns now lives, about six miles from the river, on the Cochecton and Great Bend Turnpike.

Skinner Family

Joseph Skinner was one of the proprietors under the Yankee purchase of July 11, 1754. Under this purchase and another under the sanction of the Colony of East Jersey, the Skinner family came into the country to seek their fortunes and make settlements.[4] In 1755 Joseph Skinner was on the Delaware River on what was then called by the Indians Ackhake Place, meaning Wolf Place, the farm where George Bush now lives. Joseph Skinner gave his son Daniel a deed in the following words:

"To all persons to whom these presents shall come: Greeting: Know ye that I, Joseph Skinner, formerly of Canterbury in New England, in Windham County, and Colony of Connecticut, now on the late Purchase on the West side of the Delaware River; for and in consideration of five pounds current money of the Province of New York, to my full content by Daniel Skinner on said Purchase, do give, grant, sell, and convey, to the said Daniel Skinner, his heirs, executors, and administrators, to the one-fourth part of the one hundred acres of land purchased on the West side of the Delaware River Archape [Ackhake] Place in quality and quantity. Furthermore, I do the said Joseph Skinner, his heirs, executors, and administrators, aquaint [quit] claim by me or any one, under me whatsoever. Witness my hand and seal this 8th Day of September, 1755.

Delivered in presence of Joseph Skinner, Benj. Ashley,[5] Wm. Price." The Wm. Price who signed this paper, as near as I can learn, was a surveyor, then in the employ of the Connecticut Company.

Some time after, Joseph Skinner went from here for the purpose of making some arrangements relative to the pur-

2

chase, or title, and did not return. His wife, not being the mother of his children, after waiting a length of time, concluded he was dead, and returned to her relatives at Canterbury, Connecticut, where she came from. He was afterwards found dead, about two miles from his home, being shot by some one unknown.[6] He was recognized by a prayer book found in his pocket, in which his name was written.

Daniel Skinner, the son of Joseph Skinner, was born in the town of Preston, County of Windham, Colony of Connecticut on March 22, 1733. He had seven brothers[7] and two sisters, viz: Benjamin, Timothy, John, Abner, Haggai, Calvin, Joseph, Martha, and Huldah. He assisted in laying out the town, the center of which was about six miles from the river, and also assisted in selecting a location for a meeting house and a lot for their minister. After the purchase of land from his father he made his home principally at the Ackhake Place till after his father was killed. About the year 1759, he took up residence in Newtown, Sussex County, New Jersey.

As buckskin breeches and check flannel shirts were altogether the fashion in those days, and as skins could be had very cheap of the Indians, where Daniel Skinner then resided, and he could get checked flannel of the Yankees where he came from, he followed peddling these articles throughout the settled parts of Pennsylvania and New York. Thereby he became acquainted with most of the inhabitants of these states.

Benjamin Skinner, Joseph Skinner's oldest son, having a family of boys old enough to labor, commenced a settlement near the center of the laid-out town of Cochecton. Sometime between 1755 and 1762, Abner, Haggai, and Calvin Skinner made some improvements at the river. Timothy Skinner was a millwright, and in 1757 assisted Simeon Calkin and others in building a grist mill and saw mill at Cushetunk on Calkin's Creek, nearly opposite the north end of Beach's tannery, at Milanville.

In 1756 Daniel Skinner purchased a half right in the Susquehanna Purchase for four pounds to Timothy Kinne. On the 2nd of January, 1760, Daniel Skinner, now a resident of Newtown, Sussex County, New Jersey, paid four pounds to Timothy Wints of Canterbury, Connecticut, for half a share in the Delaware Purchase.[8] On the 20th of February, 1760, he paid to Alpheus Gustin of Newtown, New Jersey, five pounds for one-fourth right in the Delaware Purchase, lying on both sides of the Delaware River, one hundred acres thereof being laid out in the middle township, Alpheus Gustin being a proprietor.[9] On the 26th day of July, 1760, Daniel Skinner paid to Benjamin Skinner of Newtown, forty pounds for one-half right in the Susquehanna Purchase, which right Benjamin had originally purchased of Joseph Skinner who, being a proprietor, had had a whole right.

This year Daniel Skinner became a sailor and made a voyage to several of the West India Islands. On March 11th, 1761, he married a widow by the name of Lillie Richardson. They were married in Pomfret, Connecticut, by Jeremiah Hinna. His wife was born in Preston, Connecticut, November 11, 1731. Her mother died when she was a child and, being very poor, she was taken and brought up by a certain doctor. Her father went into the army against the French and was killed at Cape Breton, in besieging Louisburg, May, 1745.[10] She continued with this doctor until she was between fourteen and fifteen years of age. In the meantime her employment had been such as to keep all her faculties, both corporal and mental, in active operation, so that when she left the doctor she was a heroine prepared to encounter anything hard and rugged when she should be attacked. It is said that she was very beautiful. In consequence she had many gallants, but she was poor, also, and so very few were willing to make her a wife. However, she found a man by the name of Richardson as poor as herself, to whom she was married, and, after living with him for a suitable time, she bore a daughter, Phoebe. About 1755 Richardson went into the army and was killed at Braddock's defeat.[11] At this time, having an older sister who was married and in comfortable circumstances, she made her home with this sister until she married Daniel Skinner. Her daughter Phoebe at the time was about seven years old. After his marriage Daniel Skinner then moved to a place called Manbroken; he stayed there about eight months and then moved to New Windsor.

From a document still on file in Northampton County dated 8th of June, 1761, Wm. Allen, Chief Justice of the Province of Pennsylvania, ordered the Sheriff of Northampton County to arrest Daniel Skinner, Timothy Skinner, Sim[e]on Calkin, John Smith, Jeddediah Willis, James Adams, Irwin [or Ervin] Evans, and others for having intruded on the

4

Indian lands about Cushetunk; to take up such Connecticut men, and others, as have settled about Cushetunk without leave.[12] I presume this was of such a nature that it could be served on men when they could not be found, as well as when they could be found, and was only a preparatory measure for that which afterwards took place. I could never learn that this order was acted upon.[13] This, I imagine, was the reason that prevented Skinner from moving to Cochecton immediately after he was married. Nevertheless Simeon Calkin and Timothy Skinner left the country and never returned. How many more left I have never learned. Aaron and Moses Thomas (I) took their place.[14]

On the 19th of November, 1761, Daniel Skinner paid to Benjamin Skinner fifteen pounds for one-fourth right in the Delaware Purchase.

"Dec. ye 10 A.D. 1761. Whereas we, Augustin Hunt and Thomas Corbin of New York Government have obtained a Warrant of Philadelphia Land Office for 30,000 acres of land, which is a hundred rights, three hundred acres each right, ten of which rights are allowed to be Daniel Skinner's and Company, according to the terms of said warrant with us and Company, as within our lands. Augustin Hunt, Thomas Corbin, Thomas Willing."

Indian Raid, 1763

Sometime in November, 1762 (sic), a party of Indians was sent to frighten the inhabitants, to kill, or drive them from the country.[15] They first came to the River at what is now called Milford. There they found Tom Quick's father and family and they made a prisoner of Tom, who at that time was seven years old.[16] Then they moved slowly up the river so that the people might hear of them in time if they would make their escape--their directions having been to kill or make prisoners of a few, and frighten the rest.

At that time East Jersey claimed the river to a rock known by the name of Station Rock, standing by the river about half a mile above Cochecton bridge.[17] There were two forts, one at Cochecton on the east side of the river below the bridge, the other fort at Cushetunk about one-fourth mile above Calkins Creek. The inhabitants in the vicinity of the latter were [Ezra] Witter, [Jeddediah] Willis, [John] Smith, James Adams and

5

family, Moses Thomas I and family, and Aaron Thomas and family. Whether the others had families I have never learned. The Adams family consisted of one son and two daughters, named Deliverance[18] and Elizabeth, and the other daughter was a cripple. Moses Thomas I then had children: Moses II, Elias, Cyrus, Sarah, Huldah, and Hannah. Aaron Thomas had at that time three sons and five daughters, and one that came after made six. Their names were: Aaron, Joseph, Benjamin, Dolly, Molly, Charity, Lois, Elsie, and Rachel.

Moses Thomas' home was in the blockhouse and James Adams, I presume, also lived within the fort. Aaron Thomas lived where Calvin Skinner now lives about half a mile from the fort.

There were two boys cleaning grain on the flats above Halbert's Eddy when the Indians were discovered. They were sent up the river to give the people notice. This was in the morning.[19] Calvin Skinner's wife had lately been put to bed, and he and his elder sons had gone from home. They went immediately and brought her in her bed to the fort.[20] By this time all the women and children belonging to the neighborhood were gathered in. Moses Thomas' daughter Sarah was the wife of Nat Evans and was settled at Ackhake, about six miles up the River. In order to get her out of danger Moses I sent his son Moses II and Master Fay on horseback with the order to ride with all speed to warn the people as they rode. Thus the fort was left with all the women and children of the neighborhood and with very few men. Moses Thomas I had two daughters in the fort, one named Huldah, about fifteen years old; the other, Hannah, a little rising seven years.

Bezaleel Tyler I lived in the upper settlement and had at that time ten children, the oldest twenty years, and the youngest six months. With them he made his escape through the woods. Night soon overtook them and they struck up a fire and encamped. Here they were overtaken by Nat Evans and family, Master Fay, and young Moses Thomas. They all got through safely without any incident worthy of notice.

Elias Thomas and Deliverance Adams were about fourteen years old, and being out somewhere together, hearing the alarm, they ran to the river a short distance from the fort, where they found two canoes. They took the canoes and crossed the river and made their way through the woods to Minisink.[21]

6

The Indians not coming as soon as was expected, the people supposed that they had had a false alarm. Thomas, Willis, and Witter went out of the fort to see if they could discover them, and just as they rose the bank below Calkin's Creek the Indians shot Thomas and he fell dead. Willis and Witter ran towards the fort, and as they were crossing the Creek, Willis was shot down.[22] Witter made his escape into the fort with a number of bullet holes in his clothes. He immediately closed the gate of the fort and ordered every woman and child that was able to lift a gun to hold one at the portholes. Thus were they stationed when the Indians came up. Thus standing in an open space, and near the bank of the river, there was no way in which the Indians could approach without being exposed to the fire from the fort, except under shelter of the bank.

Accordingly, after they had reconnoitered round the fort a discretionary distance, they came under the bank near the fort and asked how many men they had and were assured that they had men enough, and that they might come on as soon as they pleased, at which one of the Indians put his head above the bank. Witter, who was ready and watching, at that instant fired; the Indian fell dead and tumbled down the bank. The others, after a short time, carried him away. They were gone about an hour and a half and then returned.

While they were gone, some men from the other side of the river brought back the two canoes which the two boys had taken over. These men got into the fort before the Indians returned. The Indians, seeing the canoes, and knowing that when they went away they were on the other side of the river, reasonably supposed that a number of men had crossed the river in the canoes to reinforce the fort. Under this conviction they thought their safest way out would be to leave the country. Accordingly, they took their course up the north branch of Calkin's Creek. It was almost night, so they went a short distance up the Creek where they camped.[23]

They started early in the morning and soon came upon the clearing and discovered the cabin of the Skinner boys. The names of the three Skinner boys were Daniel, Jeptha, and Ebenezer.[24] It being yet very early they thought the boys to be still in the cabin. Accordingly, they threw off their packs, took their tomahawks in their hands, and rushed into the cabin. The Skinners, being out, had discovered them in time

7

to secrete themselves a short distance from the cabin, and as soon as the Indians entered, made their escape. These were the last of the Skinners at or near Cochecton. They all took their abode in what was called Newtown, Sussex county, East Jersey, in the vicinity of what is now called Mount Hope, Otisville. Daniel died a few years since in Sullivan County, and it was noticed in a Monticello paper that he was a hundred years old.[25]

The people in the fort started the next day to leave the country. They had not traveled far before they met a party of men coming to their relief, and they mostly returned to their habitations, where they were no more molested by the Indians until some time in 1777, when the Bryant Kane family was killed. Moses Thomas's widow, one son, and two daughters continued on and went to Goshen, and from there to Connecticut, where afterward she was married to a man named Ashley.[26]

Residents of Cochecton from the French War

Between 1755 and 1762 there were the following names at Cochecton, beginning at the upper end: Hollister, Dremore, Grant, Nathaniel Evans, Joseph Skinner, Russ, Cadoshe, Cash, Lemuel Burcham [or Burchim], Bezaleel Tyler I, Nathan Parks, Moses Thomas I, Aaron Thomas, James Adams.

These are some who were at Cochecton, New York, before and during the French War and were there at the time of the Revolutionary War, or returned and settled after it. I have several names of others who were at Cochecton before the Revolutionary War, but whether they were there before or during the French War I have not been informed.

The first at the upper bounds of Cochecton were the Hollisters; from them Hollister Creek took its name. Dremor Island took its name from a man named Dremor, who settled on it, also a rock a little above Cochecton Falls, on which rock he had some mishap. Callicoon was the Indian name for the Lurkey [Turkey] place. Joseph Ross settled a little below Callicoon, on the Jersey side of the river.[27] At the lower end of his farm there was a cove which put in behind a point of land which, when the river was high, was surrounded by water and made an eddy in the river opposite the upper end.

8

These were called Ross' Eddy, Ross' Island, and Ross' Cove. Opposite this was a small improvement made by a man by the name of Grant that was called Grant's Place. About a mile below was a flat containing about one hundred forty acres and was called by the Indians, Ackhake, meaning Wolf Place. Opposite this was a large eddy which became a general landing place, where in consequence of the land being avoided by the Indians, was called Skinner's Eddy.

At the lower end of the Eddy was an island containing about forty acres. This, being the largest in the river from Shehawken to Minisink, was called Big Island. A little above this Island a small stream entered the river. Near this stream a Dutchman lived, and it was called Russ' Brook. This Russ had a famous dog named Fidek. At the head of Russ' Brook, about a mile from the river, there is a valley of tillable land in the middle of which is a swamp, known by the name of Abram's Swamp, on account of an old Indian, who had a wigwam and had his home there. This Indian brought up a boy whom he named Canope, and it was not known who was the boy's father. Canope was about seventeen years old when the War began. After the War, and when the people had returned to their homes, Canope came to Cochecton, to see his old playmates. He had two other Indians with him, Nicholas and Benshanks. They made their home with Joseph Ross. They made famous shots at a chestnut tree across the river from the Ross home, on the Pennsylvania side. Canope was murdered.[28]

William Conklin at the commencement of the Revolutionary War lived in a small cabin made of stone beside a small brook on which a tub mill had been built opposite Big Island. A little below Conklin lived David Young.[29] He was put there by Joseph Griswold, a brewer in New York, who had purchased several tracts of land in that country. Conklin came under David Young. Young came from some part of Scotland, and had a young woman living with him named Elizabeth. What her other name was I never heard, but have heard say that she was brought up in the King's palace, and was waiter to the Queen of England. Griswold, having formed a union by marriage, sent them to Cochecton to hatch babies, till the ground, and keep possession.

Cadoshe occupied a place below Conklin. Lemuel Burcham occupied a place a little distance above where John

9

Drake now lives. There was a pond in front of his house about ten rods long and four wide, and a swamp of the same length at the upper end, both of which emptied into a small stream called Tyler's Brook, which entered into the river at what was called Tyler's Eddy, and now enters opposite Tyler's Island. Burcham's wife was Sarah, the daughter of Dr. John Calkin, and she became Aunt Sarah and he Uncle Lem. He moved at the commencement of the Revolutionary War to a place in Ulster County, New York, called New Shawangunk, now Mount Hope, and from there went to Fishkill. Afterwards he moved to Connecticut, where he had come from.

The next settler, a mile below on the Pennsylvania side, was Bezaleel Tyler II. There is nothing famous about this place except the murder of Joseph Skinner on his return from a treaty relating to their titles. Bezaleel Tyler II was killed at the battle of Lackawack.[30] His wife moved back in 1782, and died there in March, 1783. Simeon Bush occupied the same place, and the stream that entered into the river there was called Bush's Creek.

Bezaleel Tyler Family

A history of the Tyler family would, I am willing to say, constitute all the families of the U.S., from the old French War to the present day. Bezaleel Tyler I, the head of this family, was born in the Colony of Connecticut, November, 1716, and died at Cochecton in 1796 by drinking pearl-ash. His wife's name was Sarah, a daughter of Deacon John Calkin, and sister to Dr. John Calkin. She was born in Connecticut, August 16, 1727. She bore to her husband twenty-two children, fourteen of whom became heads of families. She had her first child when 16 and her last when she was 42. Those of the fourteen were as follows: Hannah, born 1743; Bezaleel II, born 1745; Sarah, born 1749; Silas, born 1749; Paul, born 1751; Abigail, born 1753; Timothy, born 1755; Nathaniel, born 1756; William, born 1758; Charles, born 1762; Molly, born ---; Rebecca; Sophia; and Amos--dates given later.

Hannah Tyler married Nathan Chapman. He moved to Niagara about 1784. They had two daughters, young women at the time of this removal, named Lucy and Polly. They made a halt in their moving at Genessee, where a gentleman by the name of Allen fell in love with the eldest and married her. He was very rich, and had two squaws that he lived with, and two daughters which he sent to Philadelphia to be educated.[31]

Bezaleel Tyler II married Abigail, daughter of Dr. John O. [Oliver] Calkin. She had been half-married before and had a son she called Simeon Bush. She bore to Tyler four sons and two daughters: John, Phoebe, Oliver, Elam, Moses, and Abigail. Dr. Calkin was killed July 23, 1779, in the famous battle of Lakawaxen [Minisink].[32] John Tyler married Yenachee [or Yeneachy] Vancy [or Vance] of Minisink. Phoebe married Joseph Thomas. Oliver married Elizabeth Comfort. Moses married Sarah Ross, the daughter of James Ross. Abigail married Joseph Mitchell. Elam died in youth. Simeon Bush, the step-son of Bezaleel Tyler II, married Hannah Smith of Orange County, New York.

Sarah Tyler, the third child of Bezaleel Tyler I, married John Lassely. She bore children: Cornelius; Sarah, who married David Parks; Katy Lassely married John Beamer; Esther Lassely married Mr. Salisbury.

Silas Tyler, the fourth child of Bezaleel Tyler I, married Gelosha Scott, a cousin of the famous General Scott. She bore him four sons and seven daughters, namely: Bezaleel, Able, Nathaniel, Charles, Lois (who married Enoch Owen), Abigail, Rachel, Hannah, Phoebe, Lillie, and Polly Tyler (who was accidentally shot by her brother when about three years old). Silas Tyler started to move to Niagara, New York, about 1785, but stopped somewhere this side of that place. Here one of his daughters got married to a man who afterward was concerned in robbing and murdering a man named Street. Silas Tyler, not liking the place as well as he had expected to, moved on to Niagara. Not finding a place to suit him there, he moved back to his first stopping place; here his daughter Lois married. Shortly after this, Silas Tyler moved back to Cochecton and built a house of slabs a little below Eli Bush's by the side of the river. Soon his daughter Lois, with her husband Enoch Owen, came and lived in the same house with them, where they begat sons and daughters and made improvements. Mr. Owen, like Nimrod, was a mighty hunter, and afterward became a preacher. Bezaleel Tyler, son of Silas, married Katy Shepherd and Elizabeth Appleman; both these wives were from Minisink and bore him sons and daughters. Abigail Tyler, daughter of Silas, married James Rible, a

11

famous weaver; someone hung him by bending down a sapling and fastening a withe about his neck. Able Tyler, son of Silas, married Harriet Quick and moved to Chemung. Phoebe, daughter of Silas, married Enos Hedden. Hannah, daughter of Silas Tyler, married William Edward. Rachel, daughter of Silas Tyler, married John Lane. Lillie Tyler, daughter of Silas, married John Wainright.

Paul Tyler, born 1751, son of Bezaleel Tyler I, married Hester Brink of Minisink. The children were: Elizabeth, who married Moses Van ---; Sarah; Abigail; Sophia; Polly; William; Amos; Timothy [this does not coincide with the list given later in the manuscript].

Abigail Tyler, daughter of Bezaleel Tyler I, married Moses Thomas II. The children were: Ruth, Sarah, Moses and Hannah. This Moses was killed at the battle of Lackawaxan, July 23, 1779.[33] His widow married Jesse Drake and the Drake children were Charles, Jesse, Christina, and Martha.[34]

Timothy Tyler, son of Bezaleel I, married Rachel Meddogh. William Tyler, son of Bezaleel I, married Peggy Ross. The children were: Rockram, Bill, and others.

Charles Tyler, son of Bezaleel Tyler I, married Rachel Conklin, daughter of Nicholas Conklin; she died after bearing a son, Bezaleel Tyler. This Charles Tyler married (2nd) Esabel [Isabel] Young. The children: David, Thomas, Elizabeth, John, Olida, Lina, Martha.

Molly Tyler, daughter of Bezaleel I, married George Smith. Sophia Tyler, daughter of Bezaleel Tyler I, married John Ross. Rebecca Tyler, daughter of Bezaleel I, married Thomas Barnes.

Daniel Skinner Family at Cochecton, 1764-1767

Early in the spring of 1763 we find Daniel Skinner again at Cochecton at the same Ackhake Place where his father first settled.[35] While he had been a sailor he learned the value of masts and spars for ships and concluded that they might be gotten down the Delaware River to Philadelphia. Having a quantity of suitable timber on his lot, he went to work and got into the river a number of sticks suitable for ship masts. These he put adrift and followed them with a canoe. They soon ran aground, some on islands, and some on rocks, where he could not get them off, so he abandoned

12

this method and returned home. Notwithstanding, he immediately commenced and with great perseverance and labor got into the river six large ship's masts of equal lengths, hewed each end like a tenon, through which he cut a mortise about four inches square. Into this they put what they termed a spindle. This was a white oak or hickory sapling, squared to fit the mortise in the end of each. They put a pin in to keep them from slipping off. The timbers which Daniel Skinner thus put together they called a raft, and to each end he pinned a long log cross-wise, in the middle of which he fastened a pin standing perpendicularly, about ten inches long, on which he hung the oars. Being thus rigged, he hired a very tall Dutchman to go on the forward end. With this raft he arrived in Philadelphia where he sold it to the mast makers equal to his expectations. Thus rafting commenced on the Delaware River. This was about the year 1764. Shortly afterwards Daniel Skinner made another raft somewhat larger than the first one, on which Josiah Parks went as forehand. In consequence of his success others soon united, and rafting became a business on different parts of the river from Cochecton to Philadelphia. Daniel Skinner, having navigated the first raft, was constituted Lord High Admiral of all the raftsmen on the waters of the Delaware, and Josiah Parks was called Boatswain.[36] These titles they retained during their lives.

In the spring of 1767 Nat Evans, Abraham Russ, and Phineas Clark lived in a house on the ground where Judge Moses Tyler has built a house for his son. Daniel Skinner lived on the flat about eighty rods from where George Bush now lives. Evans, Russ, and Clark had made proposals to each other to unite and drive Skinner out of the country, so they would have the whole flat to themselves, and the cutting and rafting of the timber which grew on the land. But Skinner had his brother Haggai living with him, and were both pretty resolute men, whom they concluded would not give up their rights without a struggle; notwithstanding they had an anxious desire for the possessions. Yet, under these circumstances, they dreaded the struggle and could not come to a conclusion. Thus it continued for some time. At length the men all went rafting, leaving their women and children to take care at home. One pleasant afternoon in May when all nature was smiling and animation was cheerful and gay, these three ladies whom I shall designate by the titles by which they were in after years known: Aunt Sarah was Nat Evans' wife, Aunt Huldah was Abraham Russ' wife, and Mrs. Clark was Phineas Clark's wife. These notable and economical wives hated the want of courage in their husbands to drive Skinner from the country so they might have the whole flat and the privilege of rafting the lofty pines which grew on it to themselves. Aunt Huldah said to her associates, "If Skinner could be driven off we could move into his house. Russ and Evans would help Clark, and they would soon put up a house on the clearing at the lower end of the flat for you and Clark."

Mrs. Clark said, "Yes, all very good. We are fretting about the inactivity of our husbands when we have the power to put ourselves in our possession without their assistance. We are all stout women. Skinner's wife, as you know, is a little bit of a thing, and her daughter Phoebe is but a child, and if I am not mistaken, they are very cowardly. Now, all we have to do is to put their things out, and ours in. If they resist I will hold Mrs. Skinner while Huldah will throw their things out and put ours in. Then you know we will have full possession."

Thus they had accomplished their business--in their own estimation. Accordingly, without hesitation or further delay they went to work to put their scheme in operation. When they came to Skinner's house they found only Phoebe and three children, two boys and a girl, namely Reuben, about five years, Daniel, three, and Lillie, an infant about two months old. Skinner's wife had gone a short distance on some errand and had left Phoebe to take care of the house and the children. Finding the premises in this situation, the three women anticipated that there would be no resistance and fancied themselves already in possession of their delightful acquisition. But alas, how vain and transitory are the efforts of human affairs founded on their own calculations! They did not know they were fishing for a Tarter. See Psalms 2:1, Matthew 13:15, Luke 19:42.

Before I convey an adequate idea of this affair, it is necessary to describe the characters who were to commence one of the greatest conflicts ever recorded. Aunt Huldah and Aunt Sarah were sisters to Uncle Moses who was killed at the famous Battle of Lackawaxen and daughters of Moses

14

Thomas who was killed by the Indians. At the time their father was killed, Aunt Huldah lived with her father and mother. She and her sister, who in the process of time became Aunt Hannah, had to supply the place of two men and hold their muskets in the loop holes to defend the fort. Thus they became warriors. Aunt Sarah and Mrs. Clark were both stout women and famous for their warlike character. (The battle is not to the strong, nor the race to the swift.) Skinner's wife was a small woman, very quick in motion, active and upright, quick, expedient, determined to accomplish whatever she undertook. When her temper was up she feared nothing. In 1767 Phoebe was about 13; pretty strong for her age, and possessed of a portion of her mother's spunk. Now, as far as I have ability, I have described the champions whose power decided the fate of the St. Tammany Flats.[37]

The besiegers advancing to the conflict, Aunt Huldah carried out some of the things, and Phoebe carried them back in. Aunt Huldah threw out other things and Phoebe attempted to carry them back into the home. Mrs. Clark attempted to hold Phoebe, but Phoebe, with a trip of the foot which she had learned of the Yankee boys, brought Mrs. Clark heavily to the floor, clinching her at the same time by the hair of the head. Having frequently seen how the necks of chickens were wrung, Phoebe commenced the same kind of an operation on Mrs. Clark. This, together with her fall, disabled Mrs. Clark so that she appeared to be lifeless.

At this stage Skinner's wife arrived, and seeing Phoebe thus engaged, went to take her off. Aunt Huldah, supposing her intentions were all for fight, knocked her down with a stone and cut a gash in her head, which set the blood running nicely, then caught her by the hair and called on Aunt Sarah for help. Phoebe, who by this time had rendered her opponent harmless, left her and sprang to the assistance of her mother and was immediately attacked by Aunt Sarah. Now the battle began in earnest--each having a single opponent. I shall not tell of the many collisions, but this I will say: the parties were soon without hair or caps on their heads. No one knows how long this fight would have continued, or what would have been the result, had it not happened that where Skinner's wife was engaged was a small pile of ashes, which at first she thought might stop her head from bleeding. She

15

grasped a handful for that purpose, but instead of applying it to her head she crammed it into the mouth and eyes of Aunt Huldah, and perceiving instantly the effects, she repeated the potion. Now, as her mouth and eyes were well charged with this substance, Aunt Huldah could neither see nor scold, and of course was entirely unqualified to continue the fight. Under the circumstances she made her escape as soon as possible in search of water. Skinner's wife, being thus liberated, turned her attention to Phoebe and Aunt Sarah, who by this time were pretty well exhausted, and had come to an armistice until they could take breath. Mrs. Clark had recovered so that she could walk, and came forward suing for peace. Aunt Huldah shortly came back, having been to the river--which was but a short distance--and washed the ashes out of her mouth and eyes. They all sat down to talk the matter over, and to form preliminaries of peace.

Each lamented that they had lost hair and caps, and each consoled herself that the other had equally lost. The passion of revenge, and the prospect of possession, were cooled down, so that reason began to assume its empire. Each party had found out by experience that there was no pleasure in having hair pulled out that way, and that they who pulled hair must expect to have theirs pulled. See Matthew 7:2; Revelations 13:10; Matthew 26:52.

Under the present circumstances none were anxious to begin the fight again; all were losing precious blood from the ends of their noses; and the wounds in the head of Skinner's wife were bleeding profusely. What a subject for a painter--five respectable ladies, all without caps, bald-headed, their clothes in tatters, covered with blood and dust. In this posture they sat for a few minutes gazing over themselves and at each other. Then, with one accord, they applied themselves to the waters of the Delaware, not to wash away their sins after their repentance, but to wash the filth from their bodies and to staunch the blood that was still coming from their noses and heads.

While at this engagement the three besieging ladies explained their object, their prospect, their motives, acknowledging their wrong, praying for forgiveness, and promising reformation. On this Skinner's wife sent Phoebe, who had suffered least by the conflict, to the house with orders to put on the teakettle, bake a Johnny Cake, boil potatoes, roast

16

some dried eels, and cut pork. This was accomplished in due season and placed on the table, around which these ladies seated themselves and partook of these dainties with cheerfulness and harmony. In the meantime they exonerated themselves in part by throwing the blame on neighbors, A., B., and C. They also entered into a covenant of friendship, a peace which was never broken. Aunt Sarah and Skinner's wife lived within half a mile of each other for many years in perpetual harmony.[38]

Dispute with the Indians and Nat Evans, 1771-1773

Christmas Day, 1771, there was a collection of the inhabitants at the house of Nicholas Conklin, besides a number of Indians, among whom was a Tuskarora, called Captain John.[39] This Indian, in consequence of drinking too much rum, became troublesome. Daniel Skinner and his brother Haggai were also present. When he ordered them to bring him some rum (having his knife in his hand which had a short time before stabbed a man, making a gash in his arm), he was told that he already had too much and that they would not give him any more; on which he stepped forward to Daniel Skinner and thrust at him. Skinner defended the blow with one hand and knocked him down with the other; then threw his knife away, keeping him down until a rope was secured with which he tied him so that he could not do any more mischief. This soon sobered him and brought him to his senses. They kept him a short time thus secured and when he was liberated he was very friendly, expressed his gratitude to Skinner for preventing him from doing more mischief. He offered to pay for and to make satisfaction for what he had done, and laid it all to the rum that he had been drinking. He took Skinner by the hand and told him that he would always respect him and remember him as a splendid friend because he had refused to give him rum. Thus the affray ended and this pale-face and the red man got on amicably together, and it was supposed that the affair was wholly settled. All that were present were perfectly satisfied, and this would have been the case had there been none of those little-souled animals in the neighborhood who pine to hear the voice of truth proclaimed, a neighbor's virtues or another's fame.[40] Whenever this transaction was afterwards mentioned, Skin-

17

ner was applauded, especially by the Indians who always spoke in his praise and said he was the greatest and best man in Cochecton.

Some time in May, 1772, he received the following included in a letter from James Welsh in Upper Smithfield:

Easton, Apr 27, 1772.

Mr. James Welsh: Enclosed you will receive a Warrant against Daniel and Haggai Skinner for beating and wounding several Indian chiefs of the Oneida, Tuscarora & Mohawk Indians, which in its consequences may involve the Province in a bloody war with the Indians, unless the aforesaid Daniel and Haggai Skinner are brought to and consigned to punishment. You are therefore commanded to proceed to Cochecton, taking with you sufficient strength, and bring them before me to answer for their misconduct, proceeding according to law. And this you are by no means to fail in at your peril. And I do furthermore command that you will execute this said Warrant within fourteen days from the time you receive it, and make returns of your doings, therein after the execution, to me, without delay. By express order of the Governor and Council. I am Your Servant, Lewis Gordon.
(Mr. James Welsh, Constable.)

This same letter directed him to bring Nat Evans without fail.[41] This was a difficult task, as there was no authority within forty or fifty miles, and he knew that Evans had been the cause and that he would not go willingly.

Evans having discovered what he supposed was a valuable mine, Skinner agreed with a blacksmith named Cooley [42] to try Evans' ore. According to the plan, Evans was to fetch his ore in the night and work the bellows while Cooley attended to the fire in order to get sufficient heat for the melting. While they were thus employed, Skinner and his brother Haggai rushed upon Evans and, with the assistance of Cooley, bound him, put him in a canoe, and started down the river in search of a Justice of the Peace. The next day they found Abraham Van Auken before whom the said Nat Evans made this deposition:

"Sussex County, Eastward Jersey: The deposition of Nathaniel Evans before me, Abraham Van Auken, one of His Majesty's Justices of the Peace for the Province and County aforesaid. This deponent being duly sworn on the Holy Evangelist of Almighty god, saith that near the last of February, 1772, one Joseph Ross and Aaron Thomas of Schecocton did employ him to carry a letter to the Tuskarora chief Captain John, in order to raise an insurrection on some, or all, of the inhabitants of Scecocton, and said Indians. Which said letter the said Nathaniel Evans did also at the request of said Indians carry and deliver to the Governor of Pennsylvania and did also receive a letter from the Secretary of Pennsylvania directed to Captain John, and further deponent saith not.[43] Given under my hand and seal this day of May, A.D. 1772. Abraham Van Auken."

After obtaining this deposition the Skinners let Evans go; proceeded to Easton, having previously received the following recommendation:

"TO WHOM IT MAY CONCERN: Know ye that Daniel Skinner, whom is complained of for abusing the Indians, did settle with the said Indian last winter before any complaint was entered to the Chief, as can be proved by the Indian himself and others. And the Indians are free and willing that he shall stay and improve his lands as he did before. And it is something likely it was out of some ill will that the complaint was made against Daniel Skinner and his brother Haggai. And so will consequently appear, and as for the quarrel that happened on Christmas Day Last, the said Skinners were peaceably together and some other people at Nicholas Conklin's, and the Indians were there, and was something disgusted with liquor, and began with Daniel Skinner to give him some rum to drink, and said Skinner would not; and said Indian was out of humor, and struck said Skinner; and said Skinner struck said Indian back again, and it came to some head; the Indian stabbed one man; and after the Indian came to himself he acknowledged he was in the wrong and said he would make satisfaction for the damage he had done, and there would never have been any more about it if it had not been for Nathaniel Evans, as the Indians now say. This we attest to. Cochecton May 10, 1772. Nicholas Conklin, Elizabeth Conklin, William Conklin, John Lassely."

"TO ALL WHOM IT MAY CONCERN: Whereas we the subscribers are informed that Nathaniel Evans has entered a complaint to the Governor of Pennsylvania against Daniel Skinner for abusing some Indians, this is to certify that we know of no abuse given by the said Daniel Skinner to the Indians at any time. And we do further certify that said

19

Daniel Skinner as far as we know him to be, [is] an honest, industrious, and peaceable man, both to his neighbors and to the Indians. This we do certify to the Gentlemen it may concern. Minnisink, May 5, 1772. Abraham Westbrook, Anthony Westbrook, Lanas Westbrook, Leneus Westbrook, Abraham Skinner, Ceort Decker, Yohannes Decker, Johanna Midaugh, Clark Phineas [Phineas Clark], Mortimas DeCrain, Benjamin De Puy, Isaac Vanyle[?], Nicholas Conklin, Abraham Van Auken, Robert Land, Thomas Haytor, Abraham Van Auken [signed twice?], Nemiah Patterson, Samuel Gunsaler, Reuben Cooley.

When Daniel Skinner came to Easton he presented himself and papers to the proper authorities, where he found none to prosecute the complaint, and of course was honorably discharged. He then returned to Cochecton and pursued his business as before.

Skinner's Land Troubles, 1770-1777

Notwithstanding, he soon perceived his family would not long be safe at Cochecton[44] and, being discouraged in any efforts to procure a permanent title, he concluded to quit the country and try his fortunes in some other place. His brothers Timothy and Abner had purchased land from Henry Wisner of Goshen, called the Shawangunk Kill meadows. Their titles were dated December 13, 1767, and they had lived there six years, which time the title had not been discounted and, as the same Henry Wisner had in the same tract about 700 acres not sold, he purchased the same, for which he paid 300 pounds lawful money of New York. This Deed was dated June 15th 1773. His family having been living on the premises of his brother Timothy, in a house purchased for them, having moved from Cochecton some time in November, 1772.

The cause of his becoming discouraged and quitting Cochecton is as follows: about the year 1770 he concluded to take title from Pennsylvania. Accordingly he got a survey of one-hundred forty acres and prayed and petitioned the Governor to give him a grant for the same. This was opposed by James Hays, who was at that time styled a land jobber. That is, one whose business it was to find a tract of land and make out a description stating where it could be found vacant. This was called locating. Skinner having had his land surveyed under the Yankee title, it was not difficult for Hays to locate it. And as there were many at that time who wanted the same location it would sell for a large sum. Under these circumstances Hays opposed the grant to Skinner in order to sustain his claim, and made some false statements relating to the character of Skinner, into which the Council inquired, and in consequence gave him [Skinner] a Patent dated May 3, 1775.

While Daniel Skinner lived at Shawangunk his step-daughter, Phoebe Richardson, became the wife of Gershom Smith. Immediately after receiving his patent Skinner returned to Cochecton. Smith being a carpenter, Skinner took him and his wife with him, in order to build a new house. He then united with Bezaleel Tyler, bought the Hollister place, and built a saw mill on Hollister Creek. He then built his new house, to which he calculated to move his family from Shawangunk about the 1st of May, 1777, or as soon as his wife should be sufficiently recovered to bear the fatigue of the journey; she having been put to bed on the 4th of April. He was at this time living with Smith. His wife had been delivered of a son about a month before.[45]

Revolution in the Cochecton Area, 1775-1778

The province of New York contained many warm advocates of freedom, but its capital had so long been the headquarters of the British Army in America that many of the principal inhabitants were related to the British officers and had become devoted to the Royal cause. The Assembly of New York, acting under their influence, declined to choose delegates to the Continental Congress held in May, 1775, but the people, a majority of whom were actuated by different feelings, elected a Provincial Congress by whom these delegates were chosen. When the intelligence of the Lexington battle [April 19, 1775] reached the city of New York, the Sons of Liberty were aroused to action and Associations were formed consisting of one thousand men of the principal inhabitants, who bound themselves to assist in carrying out into execution whatever measure might be recommended by the Continental Congress to prevent the oppressive acts of the British Parliament.

The ministry, desirous of obtaining these important colonies in obedience, appointed Mr. Tryon to be governor over it. He had [n]ever before filled the office and was a man of address and greatly beloved by the people. He came fully empowered to gain adherents by dispensing promises and money at his discretion. The successes of his intrigues allowed Congress, which having particular reference to him, recommended that all persons whose going at large might endanger the liberties of America should be arrested and secured.[46] Pursuant to this recommendation, Committees of Safety were created to hear complaints and to judge who were proper subjects for prison.

In Peenpack, Benjamin De Puy, Philip Swartout, and Thomas Eytle were the first Committee of the town.[47] The first two were Justices of Mamakating in Ulster County. Hamanut Van Froegor became one of the Committee. This was some time in April, 1777. About this time the Peenpack Committee of Safety, in pursuance of a complaint made by a number of people who had moved from Cochecton, sent their mandate to a number of the inhabitants of Cochecton to appear at the mouth of the Mongank to show cause, if any, why they should not be imprisoned. Among those who were summoned were Francis Little, Robert Land, and Bryant Kane. Kane anticipated he would be sent to jail and kept out of the way. Little and family and Land and his wife appeared. Nicholas Conklin was called as a witness against Land, who had been a Justice of the Peace under the King. Mrs. Land put him down, shaking her fist and telling him that he was black as Hell. Notwithstanding, Land was condemned to prison, but he eluded their vigilance and made his escape.[48] . Francis Little was set at liberty, being paroled.

Mrs. Land, learning that a scouting parting was soon to come up shortly, hurried home, took her infant, then about three months old, with her oldest son, then about nineteen, and drove their cattle into the woods to keep them out of the way of the scouts and did not return until the next day.

During the last night the Kane family had been killed by the Indians and the family of Land had also been visited by the Indians, who came to the house while the occupants, consisting of two young women and two boys, viz: Phoebe; Rebecca, of fifteen; Able, seventeen; and Robert, were all asleep, and wakened them by tickling their feet with the point of a spear. A certain Chief of the Tuscaroras, called by the name of Capt. John, had been at their house, and being ever sociable and friendly, the eldest girl supposed it to be him. She held out her hand and said, "How do you do, Captain John?" The Indian asked her if she knew Captain John. She told him that she did and that she now saw that she was mistaken.

They told her that they were Mohawks, and that they had come to drive the people from the country; that she must put on her clothes and go as soon as possible, and warn the people so that they might not all be killed.

Accordingly, she went to Kane's and found them all dead except one little girl who was in a bunch of bushes wallowing in her blood, as she had been scalped. Seeing this she ran up the river to Mitchell's, gave the alarm, and then returned home. In the meantime the Indians had bound her brother Able and taken him with them, without doing any other mischief. They went to Calkin's Creek and were met by a party of Cochecton Indians who were friends to the whites and also to the cause of Liberty. They used all their endeavors to bring the boy Able back, but did not succeed. They inquired what the Indians who had him had done and were told that they had killed a woman and children and a very tall man. They hurried to the river to make report and arrived at the house of Land about the time Mrs. Land and her son John did. John, and these Indians, together with what whites and other Indians they could muster, went in immediate pursuit and overtook them at Onaquaga. Here they found them drawn up in order to battle. The parties presented their arms all ready to fire at the word, and stood in that position five or ten minutes. Then, by mutual agreement, both at once dropped the muzzles of their guns and came to a parley. After some loud talking, they came to the agreement that the boy Able should run the gauntlet and then he might be taken back. This being accomplished they returned to Cochecton.[49]

As soon as Daniel Skinner and his step-daughter Phoebe with her husband Gershom Smith got knowledge of the killing of Kane's family, they crossed the river and took to the woods, Nat Evans' wife and children having joined them. Altogether this company amounted to six souls, viz: Skinner and his oldest son; Smith, his wife, and child which was about two months old; and Mrs. Evans.[50]

23

Agreement between Settlers and Indians, 1778

Some of the inhabitants left the country and some stayed. Solomon Decker, John Lassely, Gershom Smith, and Daniel Skinner had fled for safety to a more settled part of the country.[51]

Joseph Ross, having been commissioned by Col. Hooper to take charge of the Indians whose Chief was called Manoto, these, together with the whites, concluded that, as the office of the Governor then existed, there was no more place of more safety for them than in Cochecton.[52] Under these considerations they agreed on mutual protection. The Indians agreed to watch the tribes that were unfriendly to the whites, and the whites agreed to assist the friendly Indians if there should be an attack made upon them. These were the negotiations entered into immediately after Kane's family had been killed.[53]

Under these arrangements the people went on with their farming as usual in order to raise corn, potatoes, oats, buckwheat, beans, etc. Concluding that under the foregoing agreements the Indians would no more trouble them, and that they were so far from the heart of the war that their poverty would protect them from the whites, they were left to enjoy their delusion till such time as they had performed all the labor that was necessary to the growth of their crops. When this was accomplished they of course became dangerous to the cause of Liberty to their country, and more especially to those who had a desire to gather their crops for their own use.

Raid of the Cochecton Militia under Captain Bezaleel Tyler

Those who were left, having little, supposed poverty would be sufficient security against their neighbors who had left the country before. In this, however, they were mistaken. Their crops were growing, and bid fair for a bountiful harvest. This excited desire in their patriotic neighbors who had left the country before, to reap the harvest and enjoy the benefit. There were at this time living at a place called New Tammany one of the old settlers of Cochecton (called Captain Mush by the Indians) by the name of Bezaleel Tyler.[54] This man assumed to himself the title of Captain,[55] and, having connections all in indigent circumstances, like himself, and, as the Fall stock of provisions which was accumulated at Cochecton would be a great acquisition in their starving condition, they readily put themselves under Tyler's command.

These, together with some others, under the sanction of the Committee of Safety at Peenpack marched from there to Cochecton by the old Indian path till they came to the river at Ten Mile Creek. There it does not appear that they did any mischief, but from there they murdered, burnt, and plundered all that came in their way without opposition till they came in sight of Big Island. They here discovered a party retreating before them. One man on horseback rode directly to them and asked them not to shoot for he was one of Monoto's men.[56] His name was Handy and he was well known to most of the company and especially to Captain Mush, who shot him as soon as he was near enough, took his horse, and left the man where he fell.

Captain Mush pursued Nathan Mitchell and overtook him a little above the lower part of Big Island, and made him a prisoner. He was in Indian dress.[57] The rest of the company continued their retreat across the river to Skinner's flat [Ackhake] and across the river again at the upper end to Ross's where they halted and made a stand. Captain Tyler's Company pursued them as far as Skinner's new house, where they came to a stand[still]. From there they [Captain Tyler's Company] sent a small party up opposite Ross's to ascertain, if they could, how many Indians were there. When these called and made inquiry they received the answer that they might tell Captain Mush that they would be glad if they could come on: that they should not retreat any further; that they now had force enough to meet him in a respectable manner. On receiving this answer they concluded that it would not be safe to proceed any further. After viewing Skinner's house they thought it would be a pity if it should be burned by the Indians. To prevent which they, after plundering and hiding what they could find so that they could get the goods when they could carry them more conveniently, set fire to Skinner's house, and then retreated down the river.

When they came to Big Eddy they discovered John Land and a man named Davis coming up the river in a canoe. They had been to Ten Mile Creek to mill. Captain Tyler and most of his company, being well acquainted with these men, called to them that they wanted to inquire relative to the capture and recapture of John Land's brother Able. They declared in the most solemn terms that they would do them no harm. Davis was suspicious of their intentions, and at first declined going over; but there was in Tyler's company a young man who had been a mate with Land, and as he supposed was always on friendly terms with him, and knowing no cause why he should not still be his firm friend (and not having seen him for some time), he was anxious to talk over their old affairs together, in order to renew their friendship. In this Captain Tyler's company were these about Land's age: John Conklin, Wm. Tyler, and Joseph Thomas. Then many with Captain Tyler had lived in the neighborhood with Land and Davis. So, after considerable time, by Land's persuasion, Davis consented to go near Tyler. But as soon as they were on shore they were taken and their hands tied behind their backs. They complained of this, reminded their captors of their treachery, and of the solemn promise which they had made. Their answer was abuse. John Calkin answered that there is policy in war. Moses Thomas answered by cocking his gun and putting it against the breast of John Land, and saying he could shoot him if he had leave. Land was very stubborn, but Davis was humble and pleaded earnestly that he might be suffered to see his wife and little boy once more, stating that their whole dependence was on him and that the grist in the canoe was all they had--if they took this, and took him to jail, they would immediately perish; all of which they well knew for they were well acquainted both with him and his circumstances. Notwithstanding the prize was small, yet to such men it was too valuable to part with for pity or humanity's sake, so they put one of their company aboard of the canoe to take it to Minisink and drove their prisoners before them. When they arrived at Minisink they held council in order to abuse their prisoners. They commenced with John Land because he was the youngest, and as his feelings could be the easiest excited. They demanded of him how many women and children he had murdered. To this, he gave no answer. They then put a rope about his neck, threw it over a limb and hauled him up. After hanging a few moments they let him down and asked the same question. He then said he had never killed, or even had a desire to kill, or hurt, women or children. And they all knew that these accusations were false and malicious. This provoked the tormentors, as might have been expected, and they immediately jerked him up again to the limb. This would have been his last if had not some of his playmates wished to tantalize him a little more. They continued alternately to abuse and harry him until their exertions had exhausted their strength and there was none found willing to pull the rope again. They then left him to anticipate what might happen the next morning. He, with others, was taken to the log jail, where they were shackled and handcuffed and put in jail for safe keeping.[58] Thus ended Captain Mush's first trip to Cochecton.[59]

Families Returning to Cochecton, 1783

Names of families returning to Cochecton after the Revolutionary War: Joseph and James Ross, Joseph's family of three sons and two daughters, viz: Joseph, John, Isaac, Peggy, and Jinnie. James Ross had one daughter, named Rachel, aged about two years in 1783.

Daniel Skinner had six sons and three daughters, viz: Reuben, Daniel, William, Nathan, Courtland, Lillie, Mary, and Sarah.

William Conklin had in 1783 two sons and one daughter; after had four sons and three daughters, viz: Nicholas, John, Paul, William, Elias, Hester, Abigail, Steen, Rachel, and Elizabeth.

David Young had in 1783 two sons and one daughter, and two sons after, viz: Isabel, David, Thomas, John, and George.

Bezaleel Tyler, I, had three sons and two daughters, viz: Timothy, Charles, Amos, Rebecca, Sophia.

Paul Tyler in 1783 had two daughters and one son; after had four daughters and four sons, viz: Elizabeth, Sarah, William, Paul, Amos, George, Ebenezer, Abigail, Sophia, Polly, and Catherine.

Bezaleel Tyler II was killed at the Lackawack [Minisink] battle. His widow came to Cochecton with a family consisting of four sons and two daughters, viz: John, Elam, Oliver, Moses, Phoebe, and Abigail.

Simeon Bush had one daughter in 1783, after had four daughters and four sons, viz: Hesiah, Polly, Abigail, Weighty,

Nelly, George, John, Simeon, Eli.

Oliver Calkin in 1783 had three daughters and one son, after had two sons, viz: Nellie, Weighty, Sarah, Bezaleel, Moses, and Oliver.

John Conklin did not move his family here until 1784; had then two sons and one daughter. After about ten years had one son and one daughter, viz: Yonne, Benjamin, William, Joseph, and Sarah.

Elias Conklin in 1783 had three daughters and three sons, after had three sons and one daughter, viz: Land, Betsy, Elias, Jacob, Samuel, Hannah.

Nicholas Conklin in 1783 had three daughters, viz: Stene, Rachel, and Elizabeth.

Nathan Mitchell had in 1783 four sons and two daughters, viz: Hannah, Sarah, Nathan, Joseph, John, James. Afterwards had Stephen, Abraham, Isaac, Jacob, Polly, Lydia, Jinnie, Betsy--four sons and four daughters, altogether, fourteen.

Moses Thomas was killed at the Lackawack [Minisink] battle, but his wife returned with one son and three daughters, viz: Sarah, Hannah, Ruth, and Moses III. She was then the wife of Jesse Drake, to whom she bore two sons and two daughters, viz: Charles, Jesse, Teeney, Patty.

John Tyler, shortly after the close of the Revolutionary War, married Yenechy Vance. She bore him four sons and two daughters, and he died with the colic. Their names were: Moses, Bezaleel, Benjamin, Oliver, Abigail, and Lydia.

None of the Land family came back here to stay but John Land. Shortly after he took Lillie Skinner to wife. She bore him: Phoebe, Robert, Lillie, William, John, Marsy, Polly, and Rebecca Marschel.

In 1783 the names on the Pennsylvania side of the river were as follows: Hollister Creek, Widow Hollister Place and Grant's Place, Ackhake Place, or Skinner's Cove, Aunt Nab's Place, Parks' Brook, Cash's Creek, Uncle Jesse's Place, Calkin's Creek, Cochecton Falls, Uncle John Lassely's Place, Solomon Decker's Place, and Horse Island.

On the Jersey side of the river: Dremer Island, Callicoon, Plum Island, Ross Place, Island, and Cove, Russ Brook, Abram's Swamp,[60] Big Rock in Benical, Big Island, Bill Conklin's Place and Brook, Tyler's Plum Island, Grandfather Tyler and Uncle Paul's Place, Laurel Swamp, Dug Road,

Station Rock, Old Fort, Conklin Place, Cosheth, Mitchell Brook and Place, Bryant Kane Place--this is opposite Cochecton Falls and the last on the Jersey side. The foregoing names constitute what is now called Cochecton.

If my life and health is continued long enough I intend to tell all I have learned and knew about Cochecton, and something about Tom Quick and his associates (because our authorities did not hang Tom Quick and his associates for murdering Canope, the Indian); and about Joseph Ross, Josiah Parks, the old Boatswain; old Admiral Skinner the raftsman; old Nicholas Conklin; David Young; Nathan Mitchell; Bryant Kane, the reputed Tory; and John Land the Old Tory. But more particularly about Aunt Nab and Aunt Huldah and Uncle Russ and his son Cyrus, who were killed by the Indians near Fort Pet [Pitt][61] about-

Here ends the manuscript.

NOTES

(References mentioned in the Notes are found at the end)

1. Nathan Skinner places the southern limit of Cochecton about a mile south of Cochecton (now Skinners) Falls in one place and at Horse Island in another. Quinlan (Sullivan County, p. 183) places it even farther south, at Ten Mile Creek. Cushetunk was the original name for Calkin's Creek, and Nathan Skinner's definition, "foaming water," agrees with William Beauchamp's (p. 57) preferred meaning: kussitchuan [or ksch-itchuan], "a rapid stream." Other authors have translated Cushetunk (or Cochecton) as Cushnuntunk or "low grounds" (ibid., p. 227). Skinner seems to imply that the name Cochecton was derived from Cosheth.

2. In May, 1753, the General Assembly of Connecticut heard a proposal from Connecticut residents for westward expansion. A memorial from ninety-two residents of the colony said, in part, as follows:

> whereas, there is a large quantity of land lying upon a river called Susquehanna, and also at a place called Quiwaumuck [Wyoming], and that there is no English inhabitant that lives on said land, nor near thereto; and the same lies about seventy miles west of Dielewey [Delaware] River, and, as we suppose, within the charter of the Colony of Connecticut, and that there is a number of Indians that live on or near the piece of land aforesaid, who lay claim to the same . . . we, the subscribers, . . . are very desirous to go and inhabit the aforesaid land. (Harvey, p. 248)

Subsequently, July 18, 1753, some two hundred and fifty men who had become interested in the affair met at Windham, Connecticut, and organized "The Susquehannah Company."

In the Spring of 1754, Timothy Woodbridge was offered a whole share in the Susquehannah Company if he would become "an agent for the Company agreed for the Susquehanna purchase to order, act, and transact the whole affair of said purchase with the chiefs of the Indians that are the native proprietors of the land proposed by said Company to be purchased" (Egle, p. 15; see also Boyd 1, p. 45). Timothy Woodbridge, born in 1709, was the son of Rev. John and Jemima (Eliot) Woodbridge. He was the great-grandson of Rev. John Eliot, the early "Apostle to the Indians" of New England and was himself a teacher in the Indian mission-school at Great Barrington, later Stockbridge, Massachusetts, since the Autumn of 1735. Through his work at Stockbridge, Woodbridge became acquainted with many of the Six Nations Iroquois who lived at Onaquaga, New York Colony (then strictly Indian territory), and introduced a missionary, Gideon Hawley, to that town in the Spring of 1753.

Woodbridge delegated the actual purchase of land for the Susquehannah Company to John Henry Lydius, an Indian trader of Albany (Boyd 1, p. lxxii-lxxiv). Lydius was the son of the Rev. Johannes Lydius, domine of the Dutch church in Albany from 1700 until his death in 1710. Rev. Lydius worked with many of the Christian Mohawks of the time and was well regarded by them. His son, however, had a more checkered career, marrying a half-French Caughnawaga Indian, being thrown out of French Canada on the suspicion of being a secret Protestant and incurring the suspicion of officials in Albany of being a secret Roman Catholic. He was William Johnson's agent in the latter's early years in the Mohawk valley, but later became Johnson's rival in the fur trade. A more complete biographical mention of Lydius is found in Sullivan et al. 1, p. 645. See also O'Callaghan and Fernow 6, p. 659, and Hamilton, p. 63 and 343.

The Governor of Connecticut, meanwhile, apprised the lieutenant governor and council of Pennsylvania of the Susquehannah Company's intentions. Pennsylvania's officials reacted by sending warnings to their official interpreter, Conrad Weiser, and to the influential New York Indian Commissioner, William Johnson: "His Honour [Lt. Governor Hamilton of Pennsylvania] once intended to send Mr. Weiser to Onondago to put the Indians on their guard against being imposed on by the Agents of Connecticut for a Grant of Lands within this Province, but Mr. Weiser, who was consulted thereon, thinking it would be better to transact the Business at Albany. He dropped that intention and wrote . . . to Col. Johnson" (Pa. Col. Rec. 5, p. 771-774; see also Boyd 1, p. 71).

The Albany Congress, composed of the representatives of seven of the colonies, met in July 1754 to discuss French intrusions. On July 15, 1754, Hendrick Peters, Mohawk chief and speaker for the Six Nations of the Iroquois, declared, "We will never part with the land at Shamokin and Wyomink . . ." (Harvey, p. 268). Shamokin is located where the north branch of the Susquehanna joins the west branch. The Iroquois claimed sovereignty over this territory, but the Delawares (Lenni Lenape) and Shawnees lived in the Wyoming Valley along the Susquehanna. To forestall the Susquehannah Company's purchase, Pennsylvania agents got a deed from the Six Nations on July 9, 1754 (Pa. Col. Rec. 6, p. 124-127).

Nonetheless, eighteen of the principal chiefs of the Six Nations Iroquois affixed their signs to a deed to the Susquehannah Company dated July 11, 1754 (though actually signed at various later dates). About six hundred and fifty residents of Connecticut signed, along with a few residents of other colonies. (Copies of this deed appear in Harvey, p. 271-276, Boyd 1, p. 101-121, and Sullivan et al. 1, p. 405.)

A Pennsylvania agent, Daniel Claus, claimed that the deed had been obtained by fraudulent means, principally by getting the chiefs drunk before having them sign it or by not telling the illiterate Iroquois what was written on the document (Hazard 2, p. 174-176; Boyd 1, p. 130-133).

In September, 1762, Lt. Governor James Hamilton of Pennsylvania asked the Iroquois chiefs whether they had sold the lands at Wyoming and Cushetunk or not. Without consulting any of the other chiefs, Thomas King, an Oneida, answered the Lieutenant Governor that the New Englanders bought the lands for 2000 dollars of private Indians but not of the central council of the Iroquois; therefore their deeds were invalid. He added that the lands at Cushetunk belonged to the Delawares, meaning the Minisink Indians (Sullivan et al. 10, p. 537-538). King was later made to retract his statement that the Minisink Indians held the lands at Cushetunk, because the Iroquois claimed all lands occupied by their "nephews," the Delawares.

This conflict over the sovereignty would cause much

strife and bloodshed for the settlers in both the Susquehanna and Delaware river valleys.

3. The book Nathan Skinner refers to is Isaac A. Chapman's work, published in 1830. It was the first history of the Wyoming Valley and the Connecticut settlers in Pennsylvania. Chapman does not quote his sources, but the following report is found in the Minutes of the Provincial Council of Pennsylvania (Pa. Col. Rec.):

After arriving at Cushetunk on October 11, 1760, Aaron DePui, Lewis Klotz, John Moore, and Lewis Gordon report that

> . . . at Cushetunk have erected three townships, each of which is to extend in length on the Delaware ten miles, and in breadth, eight miles. In the middle township a large town is laid out, consisting of eighty and odd lots--two hundred acres in each lot--in each of which a water lot of ten acres appertains. On the lowlands are built three log houses, one sawmill, one grist-mill almost finished, and about thirty cabins for working people. Their number at present is about twenty men, besides women and children. About twenty more are gone home for want of provisions--but they are in full expectation to be joined by one hundred families, at least, in the Spring . . . the lands are sold for eight or ten dollars in hand for two hundred acres--twelve whereof to be cleared and improved and a house built in three years; otherwise, to be forfeited. . . . Here follow the names of some of the Committee who are also proprietors viz. Isaac Tracey, Jabez Fitch, John Curtis, Elisha Tracey, Benjamin Parks, Peabody (Surveyor), Moses Thomas, Benjamin Geers, Hezekiah Huntington, Stephen Kinney [Kinne], Robert Kinsman, John Burchard. Here follow the names of some of the Settlers: Stanton, Trim, Daniel Skinner, Timothy Skinner [Daniel and Timothy Skinner's names

were omitted in the Historical Society of Pennsylvania's Connecticut Claims papers 1, 7], Simon Corkins [Simeon Calkin] (who hath been a Justice and a Lieutenant in Connecticut, a busy fellow and a ringleader), Holly, John Smith, John Corkins [Calkin], Jedediah Willis, Jedediah Willis Jr., James Adams, Benjamin Ashley, John Smith, Nathan Chapman, Dr. Payne, Kellick. (Pa. Col. Rec. 8, p. 564; also Boyd 2, p. 29-32)

4. Joseph Skinner's name appears on the July 11, 1754, deed as a resident of the Government of Pennsylvania. Not long after the signing of the July 11 deed, others from Connecticut calling themselves "The Delaware Company" (or the First Delaware Company) signed a deed with the Delaware tribe, "in circumstances even more obscure than those surrounding the Albany purchase" (Boyd 1, p. lxxxviii). The first of these deeds (ibid., p. 196-200), dated December 20, 1754, conveyed land on the east side of the Delaware River to one hundred and four white men, including many mentioned in The Nathan Skinner Manuscript, such as Moses and Aaron Thomas, and Joseph, Benjamin, Daniel, Abner, Timothy, and Gideon Skinner. The Indian signers were Noleatock, Wessawell, Clark, Mactkka, and Pollatick, all unfamiliar names but identified in the deed as members of the Delaware Nation.

The second Delaware Company deed, executed May 6, 1755, by sixteen equally obscure sachems of the Delawares, transferred all lands between the Susquehannah Company's eastern border and the Delaware River to many of the same whites mentioned in the first deed. The third deed, dated October 29, 1755, embraced the northern half of the 42nd parallel between the Delaware and the east line of the Susquehannah Company. Its grantees included Benjamin Ashley and was signed at Coshaiton (Cochecton) on November 11 of that year by Meehockenous, Kalestias, Mackeus, and Wessollong (Boyd 1, p. lxxxviii, 308-314).

5. Benjamin Ashley's presence as a witness on Joseph Skinner's deed of land at Ackhake Place to his son Daniel deserves some explanation. Ashley was probably living at

Onaquaga (New York) when the Skinner deed was signed. His presence in Indian territory was ultimately the result of his marriage to his second wife, Rebecca Kellogg.

> Capt. Benjamin Ashley (Jonathan[3] David[2] Robert[1]), b. 9 February 1714-5 in Westfield, Mass., . . . married, 1st, 17 May 1739 in Westfield, Susannah Bancroft . . . married, 2d, 13 March 1744-5 in Suffield, Conn., Rebecca Kellogg, daughter of Capt. Martin and Sarah (Lane nee Dickinson) Kellogg, born 22 December 1695 (Trowbridge, p. 67)

> [Rebecca Kellogg] was the youngest of the [Kellogg] children captured by the Indians, when Deerfield was destroyed [February 29, 1704], and resided with them in Canada until a grown woman, and became acquainted with their language. She returned to New England about 1728. Her brother, Joseph, presented a memorial to the General Court in that year, showing that: "With much persuasion, he has brought his sister from Canada, being obliged to take an Indian man and boy with whom she lived to make her easy, and to promise that he would use no force with her to keep her from returning to Canada, she being besotted to the Roman Catholic religion, praying that the said Indians may be sent away in such a manner as may be for their satisfaction, and the Court may use their authority to prevent his sister's return." (Hopkins 1, p. 63)

At the time of their marriage, Rebecca Kellogg was an aging spinster of 50 and Benjamin Ashley only age 30. Benjamin and Rebecca Ashley became teachers in the Indian school in Stockbridge about 1752, "she being employed as an interpreter" (Trowbridge, p. 67). In February, 1752, Gideon Hawley became a co-worker of theirs at the Stockbridge school. In an autobiographical letter written in 1794, Hawley said that he "was instructor of a few families of Iroquois who

36

came down from their country for the sake of Christian knowledge and the schooling of their children. These families consisted of Mohawks, Oneidas, and Tuscaroras from Canajoharie and Oghwaga [Onaquaga]" (Harvey, p. 257).

> Jonathan Edwards, at that time minister of Stockbridge and missionary to the Indians, took a deep interest in the welfare of the Indians at Onaquaga on the Susquehanna River, and procured a missionary for them, Rev. Gideon Hawley, who was accompanied by Captain and Mrs. Ashley. They started on May 22, 1753, and proceded [sic] to Schoharie, thence to the Susquehanna River, and down it to the Onnohoghwage [Onaquaga] Indians near the Great Bend in the Susquehanna. They labored here, with satisfactory results, until the death of Mrs. Ashley in 1757. (Trowbridge, p. 67-68)

Benjamin Ashley's name is included as a resident of the Province of New York in the 11 July 1754 deed between the Six Nations chiefs and the Susquehannah Company, and it was from Onaquaga that Joseph Skinner was making his way when murdered in December, 1755 (see following note). The second time Benjamin Ashley appears in Nathan Skinner's manuscript is discussed in note 26.

6. The only contemporary report of Joseph Skinner's death is found in the Rev. Gideon Hawley's diary, kept while the missionary resided at Onaquaga, New York. It says:

> Wednesday, 16 December, 1755. I sent large accounts of affairs here to Mr. Oliver which I enclosed to Lt. Pitkin Esquire of Hartford by Mr. Skinner and Hooss.

> Saturday, 26 December, 1755. This week had news that Conshethton [Cochecton] is destroyed and that Skinner and Hoos, who left us on Thursday last week, are both killed but hardly believe it. Hope it is not true. (Micro-

film of Hawley diary from Broome Cty. N.Y., Historical Association.)

In a footnote to the December 16 entry Hawley writes: "The men who took this letter were both killed by the Indians and the letter fell into the hands of the French a few days after" (ibid.). It would thus appear that the Indians who killed Skinner were pro-French.

In early December the pro-French Tioga Delawares had received messengers from the Six Nations who demanded that the Delawares lay down the hatchet and repair to a council fire at Onondaga, because the Iroquois did not want the Delawares to continue raiding the English settlers. According to Anthony F. C. Wallace (p. 83-84), the Delaware chief Teedyuscung led a scalping raid (the only one he ever conducted in person) soon after the Six Nations messengers had departed. By New Year's Eve, Teedyuscung and his warriors reached the settlements north of the Kittatinnies, close to the Delaware River. While their path has not been mapped, it is possible that Teedyuscung's war party swung wide enough, in getting to the Delaware, to kill Skinner (and Hooss) enroute.

7.   Several of these brothers immigrated to Upper Canada after the Revolutionary War. After leaving Cushetunk, Timothy Skinner lived in Sussex County, New Jersey. During the Revolution he was imprisoned for fourteen months and fined 168 Pounds by the state of New Jersey for being a Loyalist. He left New Jersey in 1783 and traveled to Niagara, where he was later granted two lots on the Niagara Peninsula, as was William Skinner. Benjamin and Haggai Skinner were granted one lot each (Palmer, p. 792-793; Ontario Arch., p. 339). Benjamin Skinner was assessor of the township of Stamford, Upper Canada, in 1793, followed by Timothy Skinner in 1794. Haggai Skinner's son, another Haggai (b. 1780) settled south of Drummond's Hill by Lundy's Lane, fought for the British during the War of 1812, and is buried at Lundy's Lane (d. June 28, 1844). His sons, including Haggai Junior and Conrad (who both fought in the Union army in the Civil War), are buried beside him (Green, p. 55).

8. Quinlan (Sullivan County, p 187-188), gives the text of this grant:

> To all people to whom these presents shall come, greeting. Know ye that I Timothy Wents of Canterbury in the county of Windham and colony of Connecticut in New England practitioner of Physick for and in consideration of the sum of three pounds in lawful money paid in hand by Mr. Daniel Skinner of Newtown in Sussex County New Jersey have given, granted, bargained, allowed, conveyed, and confirmed and by these presents sell, convey, and confirm and make over and assign unto him the said Daniel Skinner and to his heirs and assigns forever one-half share or right in the Delaware Purchase of lands on the east and west sides of the Delaware River which said Wents purchased of Henry Walton, to have and to hold the same with all privileges and appurtenances thereof to him said Daniel Skinner to his heirs and assigns forever. In witness whereof I the said Timothy Wents have hereunto set my hand and seal this second day of this instant January Annoque Domine 1760.
>
> Timothy Wents
> Sealed and delivered in the presence of

us

> Nathan Clark
> Ambrose Blunt.

Timothy Wents and Timothy Kinne may be the same person. There is no further mention of Timothy Kinne, who was probably a kinsman, since Daniel Skinner's mother's maiden name was Kinne (Wahl, p. 8). The Henry Walton mentioned in the deed was one of the recipients of the December 20, 1754, deed which conveyed lands solely on the east side of the Delaware. Thus, although the deed from Timothy Wents mentions land on both sides of the river, it actually pertains only to land on the east side.

9. The text of this deed, also given by Quinlan (ibid.), is actually for one-fourth right, rather than the one-half right stated by Nathan Skinner. The land is in the middle township, and hence south of Ackhake.

To all people to whom these presents shall come, greeting. Know ye that I Alpheus Gustin of Newtown in the county of Sussex and colony of New Jersey for and in consideration of the sum of five Pound[s] lawful money of New Jersey paid in hand by Dan'l Skinner of the town and county aforesaid I have given, granted, bargained, sold, conveyed and confirmed and do by these presence sell, convey and confirm and make over and assign unto him the said Daniel Skinner and his heirs and assigns forever one fourth part of a right of land in the Delaware Purchase lying on east and west side of Delaware River one hundred acres thereof being laid out in the middle town, I being a proprietor and had a half Right in said Purchase as the Indian Deed will make it appear more fully, to have and to hold the same with all the privileges and appurtenance[s] thereof to him the said Dan'l Skinner to his heirs and assigns forever. Furthermore, I the said Alpheus Gustin do bind my heirs and assigns forever to warrant and defend said fourth part of a Right from all claims and challenges that may or shall arise by or under me or either of the proprietors of said Purchase or either of us or heirs or assigns forever. In witness whereof I the said Alpheus Gustin have hereunto set my hand and seal this twentieth day of February in the year of our Lord one thousand seven hundred and sixty. Alpheus Gustin
Signed Sealed and Delivered in the presence of
Alpheus Gustin

her
Mary X Buck
mark.

10. The attack on Fort Louisberg, situated on Cape Breton Island north of Nova Scotia, was made during what was known in America as King George's War: 1744-1748. British and American colonial forces, led by William Pepperrell of Maine, embarked from Boston on March 24, 1745, to besiege the Fort, which surrendered June 17, 1745.

11. Major General Edward Braddock arrived in Virginia in March, 1755, with two British regiments and orders to capture French-held Fort Duquesne on the Forks of the Ohio. He recruited men and supplies from Pennsylvania and Virginia (not from Connecticut) and proceeded with his British and colonial troops to within nine miles of Fort Duquesne. On July 9, 1755, these forces were ambushed and decimated by the French and their Indian allies. Over nine hundred men were killed and wounded, including every British and colonial officer save one, George Washington. The fort was captured by the British in 1758 and renamed Fort Pitt, in honor of Britain's prime minister.

12. As early as November 1757 (and possibly earlier, when Joseph Skinner was killed), the Delaware chief Teedyuscung claimed the land at Cushetunk up to Station Rock, as well as the Wyoming Valley: "Teedyuscung, in the private conference held with him by Mr. Croghan . . . produced a paper purporting to be a draught [draft] for the lands he requested might be granted to them [the Delawares] for their habitation" (Hazard 3, p. 300-301). On September 18, November 13, and December 10, 1760, the Delaware chief complained to Pennnsylvania Lt. Governor James Hamilton and his council about the settlers at Cushetunk, claiming that the Connecticut deeds had been signed by Jersey Delawares (Boyd 2, p. 24-25, 33, 35). The lieutenant governor sent the four men mentioned in note 3 to Cushetunk to report on the settlement and to notify the settlers that they were in Pennsylvania's jurisdiction and must leave (ibid., p. 29-33). In early February, 1761, hearing of "a most wicked revival of the Connecticut claims," Hamilton, "afraid [of] the renewal of the Indian war . . . sent the sheriff and some of the magistrates of that [Northampton] County to inquire into their [the settlers'] pretensions and proceedings, and to warn them off" (Sullivan et al. 10, p. 212 in Nat. Arch. Canada RG 10, v. 1824). He had scarcely sent his directive to the Northampton County sheriff when "Teedyuscung came in great concern to inform me [Hamilton] of this settlement and to insist, that the Government these people came from should be desired to recall them, and, if they did not, that I [Hamilton] should remove them, and if neither Government would do it, he assured me that the Indians would do themselves justice" (ibid.). Ten days later Hamilton issued a proclamation requiring the settlers at Cushetunk to remove themselves from the land (Harvey, p. 391).

Hamilton sent another agent, James Hyndshaw, to see what was the effect of his proclamation. Hyndshaw went to Peter Kuikendale's tavern in Sussex County, New Jersey (a favorite stopping-off place for Pennsylvania's agents) in April and was told that the Cushetunk Indians supported the Connecticut settlers. Traveling to Cushetunk, he

> put up at the house of Moses Thomas, one of the principal men of the settlement, and saw over the door an advertisement, signed Moses Thomas, giving notice to all inhabitants of the settlement that they were to meet at his, the said Thomas's house on the Monday following, in order to choose a Magistrate and their other officers for the ensuing year . . . [Hyndshaw] went and found [Moses Thomas] at work at a new erected mill for grinding corn, and entering into a conversation with him about the settlement, the said Thomas told this deponent that he wondered that Lord Penn should send up there a proclamation threatening them with the Indians; that he was settled under a Connecticut right, which he thought a good one, but if it should prove otherwise he would take and hold his land under the Lord Penn . . . That this deponent saw four houses which the said settlers had built at Cushetunk, and they told him there were other houses which he did not see, and he observed that there were a great many families in the said Moses Thomas's house,

the beds lying as thick on the floors as they commonly do in an hospital; and that he also saw there a large Block House which the said settlers were building . . . and that they intended to get some swivel guns for it. (Pa. Col. Rec. 8, p. 612-614; see also Boyd 2, p. 83-84)

Hamilton issued the arrest order quoted by Nathan Skinner soon after he received the written report from James Hyndshaw (May 7, 1761).

13. Lt. Governor Hamilton took no further action against the Connecticut settlers, but he sent another agent in May of the next year.

Information of John Williamson, who was employed by Jno. Jennings to go to Cushetunk, and gain intelligence of the numbers settled there, etc. Sixteen families are settled on the river; their whole settlement extends seven miles. Their head man is named Moses Thomas, [and] lives in ye second settlement; his brother lives half a mile from him, and is named Aaron Thomas. He lives in ye first settlement. Third Settlement: Isaac Tracey owns a sawmill, Christopher Tracey (brothers); Jonathan Tracey, their cousin, lives with Christopher; Reuben Jones lives with Isaac Tracey; Moses Kimboll, ditto; Levi Kimboll, ditto; James Pennin; Daniel Cash. Fourth settlement: Nathan Parks; Tyler; Cummins. There are in all forty Men. [They] told him [Williamson] they hold their Lands under New England--have laid out a town four miles to the west of them, on a body of fine land on a branch running in[to] Lackawaxen--threatened if any sheriff came to molest them they would tie a stone about his neck, and send him down to his Governor. They knew the woods well, and would pop them down three for one.

Nathan Chapman, who lives on the Jersey side, told him [Williamson] [that] no body of men could come up [the river] without their having notice half a day before they arrived from the Minisink people, who had promised to give them intelligence. They told him [Williamson] they had not heard from Connecticut in a great while, and did not know whether any persons were coming from thence to settle among them, but that whenever Wyoming was settled, they would leave Cushetunk and go and settle there under New England (except Nathan Park, who said he would submit to any government that had the right to it [Cushetunk]). [Williamson] was informed by them that the land held good for fifty miles up [the] Delaware. . . . Some have got four or five acres of Indian corn, some three, some two; no wheat. [They] live in pretty good log houses, covered with white pine shingles or boards; vast quantities of that kind of timber there, very fine. The land on which they are settled is very good. Did not pretend to hold under any Indian right, said it would be hard to hurt them, [they] should fall on those who sent [any officials against them]; [They] were in general scarce of Provisions--especially bread--and get their corn in canoes from Minisink. The land flies are intolerable. . . . From Kuikendalls travelled in an Indian path to Cushetunk, which is forty miles, a miserable rocky country.
June 18, 1762. (Hazard 4, p. 83-84; see also Boyd 2, p. 137-138)

Early the next year, Lt. Governor Hamilton wrote Sir William Johnson that although he himself had originally intended to remove the illegal Connecticut settlers from Cushetunk following several complaints from both the Six Nations and Delaware Indians, orders had been sent by the king to Sir Jeffrey Amherst, commander of British forces in North America, and to Governor Fitch of Connecticut to remove the

Connecticut people from the Delaware and Susquehanna valleys. On hearing of the orders to Amherst, Hamilton suspended his own removal operations until he learned what steps Sir Jeffrey proposed to take against the settlers (Sullivan et al. 10, p. 656).

Sir Jeffrey, a notorious Indian-hater, ignored the orders from his sovereign and did nothing. In the fall of 1763, the Indians, as they had promised, took the matter into their own hands.

14. This statement is somewhat misleading. Local tradition has it that Moses Thomas I (from Somers, Connecticut) had a trading post on the site of his later house as early as 1750 (Matthews, p. 444). Moses Thomas led a party of twenty families to the Delaware Valley in June, 1757. Included in this party were Simeon Calkin, Dr. John Calkin, and James Adams. Aaron Thomas and his family, and possibly Bezaleel Tyler II, came in the Spring of 1760 (Anderson, p. 37-38).

15. While "November, 1762" is the date given by Nathan Skinner for the attack on Cushetunk, considerable evidence exists that this raid was part of a larger effort to expel the Connecticut pioneers and occurred in late 1763. On October 17, 1763, Thomas King told Sir William Johnson that "a number of Delawares headed by Aanansseraquedera are assembled at Tioga and have from their body of men sent a party to Minisink some days ago as a scout, and are returned with ten scalps, and that they, being now above 200, and more daily joining them, are determined to fall upon the settlers at Cushetunk or Wyoming" (Sullivan et al. 10, p. 896-897 in Nat. Arch. Canada RG 10, v. 1827-1828). Most authors claim that the attack was led by Teedyuscung's son Captain Bull, in revenge for his father's death. Captain Bull did lead raids on a number of white settlements in eastern Pennsylvania in the Fall of 1763, beginning October 8 near Bethlehem.

> The first intimation the inhabitants of the
> eastern borders of Pennsylvania had that
> there were hostile Indians in their midst came
> to them on the 8th of October, 1763, when,
> before daybreak, "Captain Bull" and his band

attacked the house of John Stenton, on the mainroad from Bethlehem to Fort Allen . . . [subsequently many] depredations and murders were all committed within only a few miles of "Captain Bull's" ancestral home. Altogether twenty-three persons were killed and many dangerously wounded. . . . On Saturday, October 15th, . . . the settlers at Mill Creek, in Wyoming Valley, were busily engaged in their various occupations . . . unsuspicious of danger and unprepared for disaster. . . . "Captain Bull" and his warriors--increased in number to 135 since their devastating descent upon the Lehigh settlements--swooped down upon the unsuspecting people of Wyoming, and death, dispersion, and destruction quickly followed. (Harvey, p. 429 ff)

Eighteen or twenty persons were killed by the Indians that day, among them the minister, Rev. William Marsh. The fleeing settlers reached the Delaware River and "the Minisink settlements" of white people about October 21. The October 15, 1763, attack on Wyoming is often called the First Wyoming massacre.

Nathan Skinner says that the raiders first came to the Delaware River at what is now called Milford. This would have been true if they had followed the well-known Minisink Path from Wilkes-Barre in the Wyoming Valley to Minisink Island where it intersects the Delaware River Path (P. Wallace, Paths, p. 44, 101). After reaching Milford, Captain Bull appears to have followed the Delaware River Path north and probably reached Cushetunk on the river a few weeks later. Continuing north, his route appears to have followed the Delaware where it runs parallel to the Susquehanna for a number of miles. He and his band were captured at Onaquaga, New York, in late February, 1764, by Iroquois sent out by Sir William Johnson. Johnson wrote the Lords of Trade as follows:

Shortly after my letter of the 20th January I assembled the Indians to whom I had given the war-hatchet, and proposed that they should go immediately upon service against our enemies. Accordingly near 200 of them proceeded against the Delawares near the Susquehanna. On the 26th February they received information that a large party of our enemies, the Delawares, were encamped at a small distance, on their way against some of the settlements. They made an expeditious march to the encampment, which they surrounded in daybreak. Then rushing upon the Delawares, who were surprised and unable to make defense, they made them all prisoners, to the number of forty-one, and amongst them their Chief, a remarkable Indian called "Captain Bull," son to Teedyuscung, and one who has . . . led several parties against [the English] and done considerable damage during the present Indian War. (O'Callaghan and Fernow 7, p. 611; see also Day, p. 208, 296; and Kelsay, p. 100-101)

16. Tom Quick, actually Tom Quick, Junior (who later became known as "the avenger of the Delaware") was born on July 19, 1734, and would thus have been age twenty-nine in 1763, not age seven, as reported by Nathan Skinner (Quick, p. 43). Tom's father, Thomas Sr., had moved his family from Kingston, New York, to the Milford, Pennsylvania, vicinity in 1733. "Thomas Quick, Sr., continued to prosper. . . . He erected a saw mill and subsequently a grist mill, on a stream which flows into the Delaware at or near Milford" (Quinlan, Original Life, p. 14). One of Quick's mills was at the falls of the Modder Kill near where it joins the Delaware, and he exchanged furs and hides with the Indians for flour (Quick, p. 30, 32). Thomas Quick, Sr., was shot by Indians in February, 1756, while crossing the Delaware River accompanied by his son Tom and Tom's brother-in-law, William Ennis. The two younger men tried to drag Thomas Sr. to safety, but were unable to do so. On Thomas Senior's urging, they fled and left the dying man to be finished off and scalped by their pursuers (Quinlan, Original Life, p. 15-16; Quick, p. 31-32). Note that the attack on Cushetunk was, indeed, seven years

47

following the death of Thomas Quick Sr. This may account for Nathan Skinner's confusion, and his statement that Tom Quick Jr. was age seven at the time of the attack. James Eldridge Quinlan published more on the life of Tom Quick Jr. in his 1851 book, *Tom Quick The Indian Slayer and the Pioneers of Minisink and Wawarsink*, expanded from his columns published the previous year in the *Republican Watchman*. An abridged version of the 1851 book, published in 1894 under the title *The Original Life and Adventures of Tom Quick, The Indian Slayer*, failed to include some of the material relevant to Cochecton. Quinlan also included material on Tom Quick from these two books in his *History of Sullivan County*.

17. The controversy arose when a line dividing East from West Jersey was agreed upon (Quintipartite Agreement) in July, 1676, and confirmed on 27 March 1719. It was not until 1743, however, that an actual line was surveyed by John Lawrence up to Station Rock and Cushetunk (Snell, p. 41, 43). New Jersey then claimed all the land on the east side of the Delaware up to this point, while New York claimed all the land north of a line running from the mouth of the Hudson to the mouth of the Lehigh River (de Peyseter, map after p. 6). A joint commission (New York, New Jersey, and the Crown) was formed on October 7, 1769, to settle this dispute. It decided in favor of New York, giving New Jersey her present northern boundary. This was accepted by the two colonies' legislatures in 1772 and ratified by the king on September 1, 1773 (Snell, p. 158-159), which was why a New Jersey justice of the peace still claimed some authority in the Skinner-Evans dispute of that year (see the section "Dispute with the Indians and Nat Evans" in Skinner's text).

18. Deliverance Adams was born in Canterbury, Connecticut, October 20, 1751, son of James Adams and his wife Sarah. Quinlan (Sullivan County, p. 293) says that prior to the Revolutionary War, Deliverance Adams was living with John Dusinburg on the "Basket Switch" (Basket Brook empties into the Delaware north of Callicoon).

According to Revolutionary War pension files (National Archives, Washington, D.C.), Adams enlisted at Wallenpaupack, Northampton County, Pennsylvania in June, 1776, and

48

served in Capt. Abraham Shimer's company, Colonel Ephraim Martin's New Jersey regiment, at the battles of Long Island and White Plains. He enlisted again on January 1, 1777, and served three years in Captain William Judd's Company, Colonel Samuel Wylly's Connecticut Regiment.

Deliverance Adams was a resident of Mamaking town, Ulster County, New York at the time of the 1790 Federal Census. He was living in Buckingham County, Pa., on May 20, 1818, when he applied for a pension for his services in the Revolution. Quinlan also claims that Adams' wife was a Minisink Indian. His known children were Lydia, b. ca. 1775; James, b. 1785; Jonathan, b. 1790; William, b. 1794; and a daughter who married Eben Brown (see Stover).

19. Another version is given in Quinlan (Pioneers, p. 35-42), which seems, on the whole, to be more coherent and in places to make more sense than Nathan Skinner's version. Quinlan probably got much of his version from Judge Moses Thomas III, son and grandson of the Moses Thomases in this story. In 1851 Judge Thomas owned the land on which the blockhouse was built (Quinlan, Sullivan County, p. 198). Simeon Calkin helped Moses Thomas I build this blockhouse (Goodrich, p. 120).

> On the morning of the attack, Willis, who had a clearing and a log house at Big Eddy, and who had taken his family to the neighborhood of the blockhouse for safety, directed his two sons to go to his farm to winnow some buckwheat, which had been threshed. They did not wish to go, and made many excuses for staying, all of which seemed insufficient to the father, who finally compelled them to go.
>
> They had not been gone long, when they returned, and reported that a large party of Indians were coming up the river. The lads, to the vice of laziness, too often added the sin of lying; and but little if any confidence was put in their report. It was supposed that they had concocted the story they told for the purpose of getting permission to stay at home. They

persisted so earnestly, however, in saying that the Indians were coming, and seemed so anxious that preparations should be made for the coming onslaught, that finally Thomas, Witters, and Willis concluded to reconnoiter, the father, of course, informing his hopeful sons that they would be "flogged somewhat" in case no Indians were discovered. (Quinlan, Pioneers, p. 37)

20. There is some confusion about this sentence. The Meyers version of the Nathan Skinner manuscript replaces "Calvin Skinner" with "Daniel Skinner." On November 17, 1763, Daniel Skinner's wife gave birth to Daniel Skinner Jr., but there was only one "older son," and he was only two (Wahl, p. 48). If it is Daniel Skinner's wife, she wasn't at Ackhake, for she would not have been carried in a bed down to the Thomas blockhouse (or the one on the other side of the river, either). Calvin Skinner (b. April 9, 1743, married Phoebe Freeman), son of Joseph and brother of Daniel Skinner, may have had "older sons." Without additional information, we have decided to keep the original name, "Calvin Skinner," in the text. This is not the Colonel Calvin Skinner who lived at the mouth of Calkin's Creek in the next century.

21. Quinlan (Pioneers, p. 38) says that "Witters also directed two boys to go to Minisink to notify the inhabitants of his situation. One of the boys was named Elias Thomas--the other Jacob Denny, and neither was eleven years of age."

22. Thomas and his two companions proceeded somewhat incautiously down the river about half a mile when they discovered the Indians. The latter had halted in a field of turnips, which they were appropriating to their own use so far as their immediate wants prompted. The field was on a knoll or promontory, and was so situated that the enemy could not be seen by the white men until the latter were within gunshot. The moment Thomas and the others appeared, they were fired upon with deadly certainty. Thomas was killed instantly.

Willis was badly wounded, and while running towards the block house, was overtaken and slain. (ibid., p. 37)

23. Witters began to fear that he would be subjected to a regular seige, and he knew that unless he was reinforced soon, the Indians would detect his ruse and gain an entrance. Assistance could not possibly reach him from Minisink in less than two or three days, . . . As night approached, a new source of uneasiness presented itself to Witters. A considerable quantity of hay had been imprudently stacked beside the block house, and it occurred to him that if the Indians remained until evening, they would set fire to it, and thus burn his stronghold. Nor was he mistaken in conjecturing their intention. They were waiting for that purpose.

Witters instructed the women to fire their guns at a given signal, and anxiously awaited the coming of night. His determination was to watch the hay closely, and shoot every Indian who approached it, well knowing that as long as the enemy supposed that the block house was defended by a respectable force, they would not detail more than one of their number at a time to fire the stack.

As the shades of evening began to thicken, Witters saw an Indian crawling cautiously towards the hay, and making the signal, a broadside was given from the fort, Witters himself firing. With a yell, the Indian sprang upon his feet, and then fell dead. His companions soon recovered his body.

This event, it seems, effectively intimidated the Indians. They came to the conclusion that it was impossible to take the block house as long as it was defended by such a formidable force. Carrying the body of the dead savage a short distance, they buried it hastily, fearing, probably, that if the whites were reinforced, as Witters intimated they would be, they might themselves be placed on the defensive. They then returned toward the Susquehanna by the way of the Cushetunk or Calkins Creek, which runs through Judge Thomas' farm. Before they retreated, they set fire to the buildings of the neighborhood, nearly all of which were consumed. (ibid., p. 40-42)

24. These seem to be the sons of Benjamin Skinner (bp. March 7, 1731) and his wife Millicent (Wahl, p. 8), who settled on the north branch of Calkin's Creek.

25. This Daniel Skinner is buried in Eldred, New York. His tombstone gives his date of death as November 3, 1846, and his age as 100 years, 1 month, and 12 days (Meyers, p. 6).

26. The Ashley who eventually married Moses Thomas I's widow, Sarah (Horton) Thomas, is the same Benjamin Ashley found in note 5. His name is on a list of sixty-nine of the original Wyoming settlers of 1762 prepared at the request of the Pennsylvania Assembly in 1783 (Harvey, p. 403), and also on a list of settlers actually on the ground at Wyoming in 1769. His estate was probated December 20, 1778, and Sarah Ashley's on December 1, 1779 (Dorrance, p. 179). Nathaniel Evans, her son-in-law, was her administrator.

27. Joseph Ross was originally from Bound Brook, New Jersey, and came to Cochecton with his sons in the summer of 1755, holding land under the same Joseph Griswald who settled David Young and his wife in the area (Anderson, p. 35-36; Draper 17F179). By the end of the French and Indian War (1763), word of Ross's influence with the local Indians reached the British Indian Superintendent, Sir William Johnson, and Ross was made Sir William's agent for the local Cushetunk Indians. Joseph Brant is supposed to have carried messages back and forth between Ross and Sir William (J. Coleman, p. 48, 49). During the Revolution, according to nineteenth century local historian James C. Curtis, "Brant with his Mohawks took these men [Ross and David Young] and their kin friends under their especial protection--as against the Indians and Whigs, and their scouting parties from the Peenpack and Neversink Valleys" (Draper 17F179). After the war Brant tried to persuade Ross to move to the Grand River, but after making a trip there, he decided to return to Cochecton (ibid.).

28. Elsewhere Canope is referred to as Abram's grandson, who lived with his mother (whose name may have been Magdalene: Boyd 2, p. 83) at Cochecton (Draper 17F130). Canope and his mother also had a farm on the flats later owned by Judge Preston near Hancock, N.Y. (Draper 17F102). After the Revolution old Abram returned to Cookose (Deposit, N.Y.) (Draper 17F142a). Ben Shanks, a Delaware whose Indian name was Huycon, was also called Ben DeWilt (the savage, in Dutch) and Shenk's Ben before the Revolution. He was born about 1740, and was "tall, slender, and athletic; his hair was jet-black, and clubbed behind--his forehead high and wrinkled--his eyes of a fiery brown color, and sunk deep in their sockets--his nose pointed and aquiline--his front teeth remarkably broad, prominent, and white--his cheeks hollow and furrowed" (pamphlet of Hon. Charles G. DeWitt, quoted on p. 395 of Quinlan's Sullivan County; see also ibid., p. 317-318).

In 1780, Samuel Gonsalus, Ben Shanks, and three other Indians raided the house of Lt. Col. Johannes Jansen of the South Ulster County militia, killing two women and an old man (ibid., p. 395-396). Ben Shanks was part of the Loyalist and Indian raid on Warwarsing, August, 1781, where he was burned in an attempt to dry out some gunpowder over a fire (P. Smith, p. 100). On 24 September, 1781, Colonel Guy Johnson at Fort Niagara paid 30 dollars (12 pounds) to Ben Shanks upon going to the frontiers to procure intelligence (Haldimand 21767:65).

The murder of Canope is related by Quinlan in two of his works: Sullivan County, p. 317-320, and Tom Quick and the Pioneers. Canope and Shanks were fishing with a white man named Benjamin Haines of Handsome Eddy when ambushed by Tom Quick and Jacobus Chambers. Both revenge and robbery were the motives, for the Delawares had a good many valuable furs and Haines, Quick, and Chambers had plotted to kill the Indians and secure the furs for themselves. Canope was wounded by Quick's or Chambers' shots, and finished off by Haines, who clubbed him to death. Ben Shanks, or Huycon, escaped by jumping into the river and later fleeing from Quick through the forest. None of the three men were brought to trial for the murder, for Huycon had fled the country in fear of his life.

29. Nathan Skinner first says that "a little below Conklin lived David Young," and then says "Conklin came under David Young." "Below" refers to altitude, meaning, Conklin lived above the flats and Young on them--or as some sources say, on Big Island itself (Draper 17F175e). William Conklin lived "under" Young in the sense that he probably lived slightly south of Young's place.

30. The various versions of the death of Bezaleel Tyler II at the battle of Minisink are covered extensively in Leslie (p. 74, 83-84, 126, 127, 174, 195). What seems apparent is that Tyler, an experienced frontiersman, was sent on ahead with the advanced guard of the militia pursuing Joseph Brant's men and that his musket or rifle discharged accidentally, warning Brant's Indians and white volunteers of the militia's presence. Tyler was killed while retreating up the slope with the rest of the militia in the battle. One account of his death was given to his wife by her brother, Oliver Calkin: Tyler and an Indian fired at one another at the same time and both were killed.

31. Ebenezer Allen lived at Cochecton in early 1778, when he was mentioned as "one Allan," a King's man (Hastings 3, p. 193). Ebenezer Allen was one of Joseph Brant's white volunteers at the battle of Minisink (Leslie, p. 191), and was on the British Indian Service payroll as a Volunteer in 1781 and 1782 (Haldimand 21770:8). He is also listed as a sergeant of Butler's Rangers from the Cambridge District, colony of New York, indicted at Albany June 29, 1780 (Fryer and Smy, p. 56). Allen led a British party into Sussex County, New Jersey, in April, 1781 (Cruikshank, p. 91-92). In August, 1783, he delivered letters from Niagara to the Moravians at Bethlehem, Pennsylvania. After the Revolution Allen settled where the Genessee River empties into Lake Ontario, and his grist mill there, built in 1789, was the beginning of present day Rochester, New York. In 1793 Allen moved to the Thames River Valley in Upper Canada and began a settlement later known as Delaware (Grey, p. 123-124).

> This active, rough frontiersman did not "set the brightest example with respect to morals." At this time at least two of his several wives were living near the log house he had safely hidden from prying eyes atop the wooded hill, and though he was arraigned at various times on charges of blackmail, counterfeiting, forgery, and larceny before he skipped the country, no one ever bothered to charge him with polygamy. (ibid., p. 153)

Allen left Upper Canada for the United States in 1813 (ibid., p. 215). There is a letter in the Detroit Library's Burton Historical Collection concerning the education of Allen's half-breed children (Sprenger, p. 4).

32. In the original typescript, Nathan Skinner wrote: "She bore to Calkin . . . ". From the first sentence in the paragraph he obviously meant "Tyler," (see also John Tyler who married Yaneachy Vance under "Families Coming Back to Cochecton in 1783"). Skinner continues his error in assigning the Tyler children (John, Phoebe, Oliver, Moses, Abigail, and Elam) the surname Calkin. This confusion is caused by the similarity of names in these two closely related families. The true sequence appears to be as follows: Deacon John Calkin[1] had a daughter Sarah[2] and two sons, Dr. John Oliver Calkin[2] and Simeon Calkin[2]. Sarah[2] married Bezaleel Tyler I, while Dr. John Oliver Calkin[2] had a daughter, Abigail[3], who married Bezaleel Tyler II and had John[4], Phoebe[4] Oliver[4], Moses[4], Abigail[4], and Elam[4]. Dr. Calkin[2] also had a son, Oliver[3], who survived the Battle of Minisink (Draper 17F175; Clearwater, p. 162) and drowned September 18, 1787 (Wahl, p. 60). Skinner is the only one who puts Dr. John Calkin at the Battle of Minisink (he would have been rather old), so this is probably another mistake.

33. Moses Thomas II, the boy of fifteen who was sent to warn

55

his sister Sarah Thomas Evans in the Fall of 1763 when an Indian raiding party attacked the Thomas blockhouse, was farming at Cushetunk in the Spring after his father's death. He married Abigail Tyler (daughter of Bezaleel Tyler I) in 1771, and he and Abigail applied for a warrant for their land in 1775 (Anderson, p. 52, 61, 64). They had four children: Sarah, b. 1772, m. Reuben Decker; Ruth, b. November 27, 1773, m. Abram Barnes; Hannah, b. January 11, 1775, m. an Oliver Calkin; Moses III, b. Fall, 1779 after his father's death (Anderson, p. 233).

At the outbreak of the Revolution Moses Thomas, Aaron Thomas, Elias Thomas, and Nathaniel Evans wrote Zebulon Butler resolving to defend themselves against the Tories in their midst (Taylor 6, p. 324). In late May, 1778, a party of seven or eight Butler's Rangers under Charles Smith (a private, but claiming to be a British captain), came to Cushetunk for provisions. They visited Moses Thomas' house, plundered his household goods, broke his doors, and stole his grain and hogs (after butchering the latter), and carried the grain and pork away in three canoes (Hastings 3, p. 375-376). Thomas fled to the Minisink area, where he became a lieutenant in the South End regiment of the Ulster County militia (Clearwater, p. 158), and was, according to Nathan Skinner, part of Bezaleel Tyler's company in the August, 1778, raid.

Thomas enlisted October 27, 1778, serving in Colonel Jeduthan Baldwin's Regiment of Artificers as a carpenter in Capt. Peter Mills' Company (National Archives, Washington, D.C.). He served at Newburgh and West Point but became dissatisfied with his officers, hired a substitute, and went home. When Brant attacked the Delaware Valley settlements in 1779, he again enlisted as a volunteer and was killed in the battle of Minisink (Draper 9F18).

34. Two and a half years after the death of Moses Thomas II at the battle of Minisink, his widow married Asa Chapman at Goshen, New York (C. Coleman, p. 13). This marriage occurred on February 28, 1782, the same day that William Tyler, her younger brother, married Mary Vail. Both Abigail and William were siblings of the Bezaleel Tyler who died at Minisink.

Since at least April 12, 1779, when he had been admitted freeman and taken the oath of fidelity to the State of Connecticut at a town meeting of the "inhabitants of Westmoreland held at Wilkes-Barre," Asa Chapman had been a resident of Westmoreland, Litchfield County, Connecticut, a location practically synonymous with Luzerne County, Pennsylvania, some five years later. He appears as "sergeant" in a pay roll of Capt. John Franklin's militia company from April 3 to May 4, 1780. Also on this company pay roll was Joseph Thomas, cousin to Moses Thomas II (Harvey, p. 1166, 1229). Asa Chapman was a property holder at Westmoreland in 1780, for his estate was valued at 18 pounds in "A true List of the Polls and Estate of the Town of Westmoreland ratable by law on the 20th of Augt. A.D. 1780." (Joseph Thomas' was valued at 27 pounds.) Only three people were assessed at above sixty pounds, and fifty-eight people below thirty pounds, a clear sign of the poverty of the settlers after the enemy attack in July, 1778 (Harvey, p. 1254, 1255).

The marriage of Abigail (Tyler Thomas) and Asa Chapman did not last long. Perhaps this is why Nathan Skinner did not mention it.

> Hanover was the scene of another bloody deed on Monday, the 8th of July [1782]. John Jameson, and a lad, his brother [Benjamin, aged thirteen], accompanied by Asa Chapman, were riding up from Nanticoke, their residence near (now) Lee's Mills, intending to go to Wilkes-Barre. As they came opposite the Hanover meeting house, Jameson exclaimed, "There are Indians." Before he could turn his horse he received three rifle balls, and fell dead to the earth. Chapman being behind him, had time to draw the rein and turn, but was instantly wounded. Clinging to the saddle, the frightened horse bore him beyond their reach. The lad [Benjamin] being in the rear, escaped. Chapman lingered several hours, sent for his wife, and took an affectionate leave of her. Capt. Franklin cut out the ball, but it had done its office, and he presently expired. (Miner, p. 305)

On a list of those "Killed by the Salvages [sic] in Skirmishes," Chapman is shown with four children, those of his wife Abigail and her first husband. Abigail Chapman's name appears on a list of 396 petitioners to the State of New York for a tract of land situated on the Susquehanna, within the limits of New York, signed and dated at Westmoreland, February 13, 1783. Also on this list were Ephraim and Joseph Tyler, whose relationship to her has not been identified; Joseph Thomas (Moses Thomas II's cousin), and Nathaniel Evans (Harvey, p. 1315).

35. There is some question whether this is 1763, since the Daniel Skinner family does not appear to have been at Ackhake during the Indian raid. Nathan Skinner says rafting began in 1764, which would seem when the family actually returned to Ackhake. Mary Curtis, Cultural Resources Specialist for the National Park Service, says that Skinner's [first?] rafting companion was a Dutchman named Cadoshe (letter of Patricia Christian, June 2, 1992).

36. Josiah Parks was a native of New London, Connecticut, and, according to his daughter, Prudence Parks Larkin, had served on a man-of-war in the British navy fighting against the Spaniards. He was present at the British navy's taking of Havana in 1762. During the Pennamite wars he helped to build a wooden cannon (Draper 17F95a). He settled at Equinunk Island, and during the Revolution enlisted as a scout between the Hudson and the Delaware.

> But by and by in one of his desperate encounters with [the Indians and Tories] he was taken prisoner and reserved for torture, but in their absence he managed to liberate himself from the log jail they had prepared for him and traveled twenty-five or thirty miles in the night to reach the nearest post commanded by Capt. Thomas. . . . A friendly Indian informed the Boson of the intended massacre of the whites at the Wyoming Valley and the time it was to take place. He immediately left the Delaware River near Minisink and went alone on foot with no guide but his pocket

compass through an unbroken wilderness to notify the inhabitants of their approaching danger. Almost famished with hunger and fatigue he [arrived at Wyoming and] was accused of being a British spy and put in jail. He knew two men by the name of Gore that were school mates of his when boys who were then in the Valley commanding the American forces. He sent for them, told them his tale of sorrow. They embraced him kindly, set him at liberty, and warned the people of the Valley to prepare for the conflict and remove the aged and defenceless with their effects to a place of safety. The two Mr. Gores, Asa and Silas, were killed in the massacre. . . . The Boson with heavy heart and wearied limbs returned to the Delaware anxiously awaiting the news of that expected tragedy. (Draper 17F165b-c; see also 17F165; 17F173; 17F174)

Another version of this story says that the Indian who warned Parks was Canope (Draper 17F95b). Josiah Parks appeared before the Committee of Mamacotten Precinct [Peenpack] on April 17, 1778, to report that Dav'd Vaneveran of Shohankan [Shehawken, now Hancock, N.Y.] told him that "the Indians and Tories mean to strike first on Sisqueannah about Wyomah and take that place first; with the number of four thousand men, and then come through to the North River . . . [and] that Francis Elswert, Nathan Parks, Garton De Witt, and Hank Bush are gone to the Indians" (Hastings 3, p. 192-193). This agrees quite well with Prudence Parks Larkins story; Josiah must have gone on to Wyoming after making his report to the Committee. Parks seems to have been more of a spy than a scout. By 1779 Parks and his family were refugees in the Minisink area (Hastings 4, p. 683).

After the Revolution Parks returned to the Equinunk Island area. He had two sons, William and Moses, and two daughters who married Jonas and Jonathan Larkin, respectively (Draper 17F95b).

37. Quinlan's Sullivan County, p. 183-184 states:

On the banks of the river, near the present
village of Cochecton, was an Indian village of
some note, where the savages of the surrounding country met to observe their ancient
customs. Here they had their green-corn
dances, their dog festivals, their games of ball,
etc. and here according to ancient tradition,
which has been nearly lost amid the din and
whirl of modern days, lived the celebrated
Lenape sage and Yankee Saint--Tammanend,
Tammaning or Tammany. William L. Stone
says that he lived in the middle of the 17th
century: that he was a sagacious and virtuous
sachem; that in his youth he resided in the
country which is now called Delaware; and
that he afterwards settled on the banks of the
Ohio. In truth, little or nothing reliable is
known concerning this heathen saint. The
first settlers claimed that his lodge was on the
Skinner farm, and the "Admiral" loved to
designate his valley-land as St. Tammany
Flats.

In fact, the Lenape sachem Tammany (Tamanen,
Tamanans, Taminent, etc.) was one of a number of late-
seventeenth century chieftains who appears on deeds to
William Penn in 1682-3, 1692, and 1697. He controlled land
between Neshaminy and Pennypack creeks and lived at
Perkasie, Bucks County, Pennsylvania. Tammany had a
brother Weheeland (who probably succeeded him) and at
least two sons, Nicholas Yaqueekhon and Charles Quenameckquid (Weslager, p. 168).

38. The assertion of perpetual harmony seems somewhat of
an exaggeration, given the continued rivalry between Skinner
and Evans for Ackhake and the incidents detailed in the next
section. According to traditions handed down in three sepa-
rate lines of his descendants, Nat, actually Nathaniel, Evans
was part Iroquois. Extensive research by Barbara L. Covey
indicates that Nathaniel Evans was probably a grandson of
Jonathan Cayenquerego, a Mohawk sachem (hereditary chief)

of the bear clan. Jonathan Cayenquerego ("the Deer") is described by his adopted brother, Conrad Weiser, as "a noted Mohawk that can read and write in his [own] language" (P. Wallace, Weiser, p. 380). He grew up near Middleburg, New York, lived at Onaquaga, and later at Canajoharie, New York. Jonathan was a maternal uncle to Thomas King, the Onaquaga chief who condemned the settlement of the New Englanders at Cushetunk (see note 2) and the paternal uncle of Captain or Tuscarora John (see note 39). This leads us to speculate that Nathaniel Evans may have had an Indian claim to Ackhake.

Moreover, his wife appears to have been married earlier to a Mr. Holly, an early settler at Cushetunk (see note 3 and Scott, p. 152). She may have claimed land settled by her first husband.

Nathaniel Evans was one of the first of the Cochecton settlers to enlist in the American cause, in Company E, 4th Connecticut Regiment, on September 17, 1776 (National Archives, Washington, D.C.) and later served in Captain Simeon Spaulding's Independent Company, which played a notable role in the frontier warfare in the Wyoming Valley in 1778 and 1779. Wounded in the war, Evans served in a military hospital at Wyoming and remained in Luzerne County until 1788. Between 1792 and 1795 he and his family moved to Washington County, Ohio, where he remained until his death in August, 1808. More details of Evans' Revolutionary War service and later residence in Ohio can be found in Cottle (p. 69-71).

39. Though known to whites as "Tuscarora John," John Tayojaronsere (or Tayotsyaronsere) is listed as a Canajoharie Mohawk of the wolf clan in a 1760 list of Indians who accompanied Sir William Johnson to Montreal (Sullivan et al. 13, p. 175) and is referred to by Joseph Brant as "John the Mohawk" in Brant's July 29, 1779, letter to Lt. Col. Mason Bolton at Niagara (Haldimand 21760, also printed in Sullivan Campaign, p. 107-108), and appears as a Canajoharie Mohawk in their Loyalist claims ("Losses Sustained by the Mohawk Indians . . . As Valued in the Year 1775," Q Series, vol. 24, part. 2, p. 308-320, National Archives of Canada). Tuscarora John first appears (Pa. Col. Rec. 6, p. 161) bringing a report about Monocatootha (or Scaroyady) the Oneida

Half-King, from Captain Strobo, held captive at Fort Duquesne (letter dated 28th July, 1754). Strobo's letter was carried to George Croghan, the Indian agent at Auckwick, by the Mohawk Moses Contjochqua. Moses was the adopted brother of Conrad Weiser and brother-in-law of Scaroyady (see P. Wallace, Weiser, p. 365). From the records of the First Church in Albany (Holland Soc., p. 28) Tuscarora John was apparently Moses's son, baptized on 6 October 1727; his mother's name was Alida. Captain or Tuscarora John was a war chief of Onaquaga (New York) and also the son-in-law of Adam Addingquanorum, Chief Sachem of Onaquaga (see Fonda, p. 24; baptism of Moses, son of John the Indian and his wife in Vosburgh, vol. 1, pt. 1; Harvey, p. 828-830; and note 43 below). Quinlan (Sullivan County, p. 195-196) calls him a half-breed but supplies no source for this assertion.

John Tayojaronsere fought with Joseph Brant and his Mohawks (see note 59), was wounded at the Battle of Minisink (July 23, 1779) and died shortly thereafter, about August 5, 1779 (letter of Joseph Brant to Daniel Claus, August 9, 1779, Draper 9F207; Captain John Wood's Journal, Draper 9F90-91).

40. What does this last sentence mean? Literally it means there were some people who "pine to hear the voice of truth" in the neighborhood. Indeed there were, but Nathan Skinner seems to be confused at this point.

41. Does Nathan Skinner mean the letter from James Welsh in which the warrant was enclosed? What business does a constable have *sending* a warrant to those who are wanted by the law, rather than *acting on* the warrant? Or of asking for Nat Evans without a warrant? This whole procedure, as described here, is illegal.

42. Reuben Cooley, the blacksmith who helped the Skinners capture Nathaniel Evans and who signed the affidavit stating that Daniel Skinner was an "honest, industrious, and peaceable man," was probably the Cooley said to have been murdered during the Revolution by Captain Tyler's raiding party (Matthews, p. 454). Cooley had fled north along the Delaware for safety, found an abandoned cabin near Little Equinunk, and stayed there until a scout found and executed him.

Quinlan (Sullivan County, p. 194-195) says the man's name was Payne.

43. The letter which Richard Penn, governor of Pennsylvania, sent to Captain John, and the other chiefs of Onaquaga, is as follows:

Philadelphia, the 11th of April, 1772.

"Brethren,
I received your Letter dated at Onohoquage [Onaquaga], the 16th of last month, and am heartily sorry to hear of the disagreeable News you give me of the bad Behavior of two of our People last Winter, at Cashietown [Cochecton], towards a Chief of our good Brethren the Six Nations.
Brethren,
You have acted a very wise and friendly part in acquainting me with the abuse your People have received from mine, and in not resenting the Injury yourselves, by taking immediate Revenge on the men who were so wicked as to commit it. This Conduct of yours deserves great praise, and discovers a very peaceable Disposition on your part. And it is agreeable to the Rule which you and we have at all the Treaties agreed to observe, in order to prevent the least Breach in our Chain of Friendship, which is, that whenever any little accident happens, or any folly is committed between any of your People and ours, we should immediately inform each other of what has been done, that satisfaction may be given to those who are injured.
Brethren,
You very well know that the men of whom you now complain live at a very great Distance from me, and that it is difficult for me at all times to prevent such accidents, and to apprehend and punish the wicket people who occasion them. But, Brethren, you may be

fully assured that every thing shall be done on my part to give you satisfaction in this matter. *I shall send orders to the Magistrates in Northampton, to issue Warrants for this two persons who have injured you, and if they can be apprehended, to punish them as far as our Laws will allow* [our italics].
RICHARD PENN
Directed,
To Adam, Isaac, Peter and Captain John, and the other Indian Chiefs at Onohoquagey.
(Hazard 4, p. 450)

From this letter we see the inaccuracies in Nathan Skinner's version of this incident, for the original complaint to Governor Penn was sent by Adam, Isaac, Peter, and Captain John, of Onaquaga, not by Aaron Thomas or Joseph Ross, as suggested by Skinner's rendition of the Evans deposition. Obviously the chiefs were upset enough about the incident that occurred at Nicholas Conklin's to launch a very angry complaint.

44. One wonders why not. Nathan Skinner is not giving the whole story. Obviously the Onaquagan chiefs were still angry that their complaint had failed to bring Daniel and Haggai Skinner to justice.

45. This is Nathan Skinner himself, born April 4, 1777 (Wahl, p. 48) in New Jersey. Nathan married Sarah Calkin, b. August 19, 1778, daughter of Oliver and Hannah Thomas Calkin. Nathan lived on the old Calkin homestead until about 1814 and then moved to Milanville, where in 1815 he built a house that still stands. In 1820 he moved to Cochecton, New York, leaving his Milanville home to his son, Colonel Calvin Skinner. Nathan Skinner died November 15, 1856, and Sarah Calkin Skinner died May 18, 1854 (ibid.; Matthews, p. 475).

46. This particularly evasive paragraph reflects Nathan Skinner's attempts to gloss over his family's Loyalist sympathies. William Tryon assumed the office of royal governor of the colony of New York in June, 1771, after having put down insurgents, known as Regulators, in North Carolina. He was an ardent advocate of royal authority in the colonies who, early in his term of office, did try to appeal to moderate opinion in New York. When these measures collapsed after the Boston Tea Party in late 1773, Tryon's proposals grew increasingly severe. When Continental troops took over the city after 1775, Tryon fled to the *Duchess of Gordon*, in New York harbor. He returned with Sir Henry Clinton's forces in 1776 and stayed on to command the Loyalist New York militia, eventually putting into practice his ideas of desolation warfare in areas surrounding New York City. He left America in 1780. A recent full-length biography by Paul David Nelson details his career as governor in North Carolina and New York, and the state of North Carolina Historical Archives Division has published two volumes of Tryon Papers (see Powell).

47. Quinlan (Pioneers, p. 138) lists Jerardus Van Inwegen, Benjamin Depuy, -Coit, and Swartwout as the first Committee of Safety at Peenpack. Letters in Hastings (1, p. 705) confirm that Philip Swartwout was the first Chairman, and mention Thomas Kyte (not Eytle). A later letter (Hastings 3, p. 193) also mention J. R. D'Witt and Benjamin Depuy as committee members.

48. The story of Robert Land's origins are as varied as the versions of his service during the Revolutionary War. John H. Land says that he had come with his brother from England twenty-five years before the outbreak of the war (Land, p. 39-43). Matthews (p. 457) claims that "Robert Land was a son of Samuel Land, an Englishman, who first settled near Wilmington, Delaware, where he took up a tract on White Clay Creek, which he afterwards (in 1684) disposed of to John Cann. In 1763, [Robert] Land was sent to Cushetunk as a justice of the peace under the colonial government." In October, 1725, a Robert Land of Fairfield, Connecticut, sold to John Jameson (father of the Benjamin and John in note 34) 142 acres of land in the new town of Voluntown, Windham County, Connecticut (Harvey, p. 1287f). This would fit in with Campbell (p. 9), who says that Robert Land was born in New York in about 1736, lived in Connecticut, and about 1757 moved to the Delaware Valley as an employee of the Delaware

Company. Land married Phoebe Scott, an aunt of the future general Winfield Scott, "a tall dark girl" about three years older than he (ibid.). Their oldest son John was born about 1758, followed by Abigail, b. March 27, 1760; Abel; Kate, b. 1764; Phoebe, b. 1766; William; Robert, b. 1772; and Ephraim, b. 1774 (Wahl, p. 57). Ephraim was baptized in New York's Trinity Church on January 21, 1781, with his parents standing as his sponsors (NY Geneal. & Biog. Rec., p. 379), and is the ancestor of Charles Lindbergh.

Robert Land was "a man of enterprise and perserverance and his wife, who was a Scott, was a woman of uncommon endurance and ability. He settled on the property now owned by Colonel Calvin Skinner, at Milanville, Pa." (Matthews, p. 457). On 8th April, 1777, the Peenpack Committee of Safety, "upon the doleful call of our friends at Koschecton [Cochecton] for help against the growing Tory brood we thought it advisable to order Capt'n Cuddeback to march with fifteen of his men and Capt'n Newkerk with the like number to their assistance, which they did last Sabbath-Day morning But we have had no acct. as yet from [them]" (Hastings 2, p. 705). It was probably these militia troops who brought Robert Land and Francis Little to Peenpack for interrogation by the Committee.

Escaping from the Committee, Robert Land joined the famous Mohawk war chief, Joseph Brant. Able Land, his second son, probably went with him (Ont. Hist. Soc. 24, p. 84). In late June or early July, 1777, Land took a message from Brant to New York City and returned not long after (Kelsay, p. 196). He, or other Loyalists, may have been messengers for the British even before this trip, for the 8 April letter from the Peenpack Committee to New York Governor Clinton says "Sir, by the best intelligence we can receive we must conclude that there is a constant communication kept up between the two British armies by the way of Koschton [Cochecton] and the hed [head] of the Drowned Land" (Hastings 2, p. 705).

In February, 1778, Robert Land left Cochecton with letters or expresses to New York. By April it was feared that he had been captured (Hastings 3, p. 192). These fears appear to have been unfounded, but there is no further information on his activities for 1778. During his absences, the Land home was burned twice and his family attacked.

The second time, the house was burned totally, and Mrs. Land set out with her family to New York City, where she appears by May 23, 1779 (Campbell, p. 9; J. Coleman, p. 53). The final destruction of the Land house may have occurred during the November 15, 1778, raid by the Peenpack militia (see note 59). Whether Mrs. Land and the children left by themselves or with Robert Land is unknown, but he was in New York in early 1779. Robert Land set out again as a courier carrying dispatches for Niagara on March 1, 1779. Land was accompanied by Thomas Hill, Peter Mabee and a boy, Edward Hicks (W. Smith, p. 101). Passing Minisink they were spotted and tracked. Land and Edward Hicks were captured on March 13 by five militia volunteers under Captain Schott at the house of David Cartright (W. Nelson 3, p. 226; J. Coleman, p. 53). Land and Hicks were sentenced to death in a court martial conducted by General Edward Hand on March 17-19, but the boy escaped to Niagara (with the news that Land was dead). Land's sentence was commuted by General George Washington, because Land, as "an inhabitant of one of the States" was not subject to military jurisdiction (Fitzpatrick 14, p. 357-358). Land was sent to prison at Easton, where he was released on bail (paid primarily by Daniel Skinner) on September 30, 1779, because he was not on Pennsylvania's list of proscribed traitors (Campbell, p. 10).

Robert Land jumped bail and set out for British-held Niagara on May 12, 1780, with Ralph Mordon, a Quaker, and a small party of recruits intended for Joseph Brant. His party was ambushed by the Patriot militia. Mordon was captured and Land, wounded and having dropped his "knapsack, beaver hat, and cane," escaped into the darkness (J. Coleman, p. 54-55). Without Mordon, who was acting as a guide (and was later executed), Land headed back to New York City. By December 28, 1780, Land was back at Fort Niagara, when he set out with dispatches from the fort commander, Brig. General Powell, to Montreal, accompanied by a Mr. Drake (Haldimand 21760:410).

Land's career as a dispatch courier continued between Montreal and New York and Niagara. He was in New York in January, 1781, then to Niagara, and then to Montreal and back at Niagara in August, 1782 (Haldimand 21762:148). By 1784 he was farming at Niagara Falls, and in 1787 he moved to the site of present day Hamilton, Ontario. Phoebe and most of the Land children went to Nova Scotia, probably in the fall of 1783, where Phoebe and Abel received land grants. In 1789 Phoebe and her children migrated to Upper Canada by way of their old settlement on the Upper Delaware, now owned and farmed by the oldest son, John Land. Although Mrs. Land wanted John to accompany him, he decided to stay on the Delaware. Quinlan (Pioneers, p. 159-161) said that the two went to a secret place where some of their household goods had been hidden during the war and found them stolen. John Land later beat the thief with a raft withe. Robert Land was not reunited with his wife and children until 1790 (J. Coleman, p. 60).

49. The murder of Bryant Kane's family is found in all the local histories. Quinlan (Sullivan County, p. 195) interjects a slight variant: after finding the bodies of the Kane family, Phoebe runs to the house of Nicholas Conklin for safety rather than to the house of Nathan Mitchell. Given that Conklin had accused her father, this is highly unlikely. Quinlan also says that a man named Flowers had been employed by Kane to take care of his family while he was gone. Flowers was also murdered with Kane's wife and children. The apparent incongruity of Loyalist Mohawks murdering a Loyalist family is "explained" by supposing that the Indians made a mistake and were intending to murder either the Mitchells or the Conklins, who lived one and two miles, respectively, above the Kanes (Draper 17F175e; for more on this "explanation," see note 57).

Yet Matthews says, "there seems something improbable in the Land narrative [of the Kane murders]" (p. 78), and Quinlan agrees that "there is a veil of mystery about these transactions which cannot now be put aside, and therefore we will not attempt to remove it" (Quinlan, Sullivan County, p. 197). Perhaps we should try.

The Loyalist accounts, taken from the descendants of Robert Land who settled in Canada, differ in several important ways from the American ones (see Burkholder, p. 25-27 and Land, p. 39-43). In the Loyalist versions the attack on the Kane family comes in the early Fall (Burkholder says in 1778). In these versions John Land was in prison, and the Land family was warned by a mysterious Indian voice they first mistake for "Captain Jack" to go to the white man's house over the river because "He want you--bad." The Lands arrived at the Kane homestead to find the family murdered. Returning to their own home, the same mysterious voice warned them to get the children out for the house would be burned. Mrs. Land and the children then left their home and hid nearby, where they watched their home go up in flames set by a group composed of Indians and their former neighbors.

Factual information of the Kane murders at the time they occurred is nonexistent. However, Abel Land's testimony directly contradicts the traditional Nathan Skinner version. According to a petition filed by Able Land in 1795,

> In the early part of the late American War your petitioner with his father, commonly called Captain Robert Land, took arms for [the British] Government and entered upon actual service under Captain Brandt, was afterwards taken prisoner at a place called Coshecton when acting as a volunteer under the said Captain Brandt, made his escape from confinement and joined the royal standard at New York, when he entered and served in the Engineer Department. (Ontario Hist. Soc. 24, p. 84)

Unfortunately, Abel Land does not supply any dates, although he was in service as a artificer in New York City on August 26, 1781 (NYHS Col., p. 152).

Given all this conflicting information, a clearer understanding of the Kane murders rests on when they actually took place. An April, 1777, date is too early for Abel's capture as a "Brandt Volunteer," since Joseph Brant arrived at Onaquaga on April 16, and had only begun to acquire forces in late May or early June of that year. A year later, on 17 April 1778, Joseph Gordens tells the Committee of Mamacotten Precinct that the Indians and Tories would take all the Whigs at Cochecton in five weeks, "And the persons which would not be hurt that were Kings men: Viz. Joseph Ross, Nath'l Michel, Brian Cain, one Allan, Robt. Land, Dan'l Skinner, Jonas Wood, Haggai Skinner" (Hastings 3, p. 193). Thus Bryant Kane was still in Cochecton at that time.

Something of the substance in Abel Land's petition is hinted at in the Skinner account of the capture of John Land during the 10 August, 1778, raid by Captain Tyler (see following section in the text), when the raiders inquire "relative to the capture and recapture of John's brother Abel." Moreover, John Land and Nathan Mitchell, two individuals who appear in Skinner's story of the Kane murders, are captured by Captain Tyler during that raid. If Skinner's account of the Captain Tyler raid is accurate, then the capture of Abel and John Land would have taken place during or before the 10 August, 1778, raid (see note 59). That date might be taken as the early Fall, 1778 date given in the Loyalist versions of the story of the Kane murders. But the Loyalist date for the murder may have been confused by the fact that the burning of the Land house took place twice (see previous note). In the broadest terms, the murders most likely took place between mid-April and 10 August, 1778. Using the material in notes 50, 51, and especially 53, it probably took place in late June or early July of that year.

This was a very turbulent time in Cochecton's history, beginning with the appearance of Ranger Charles Smith at Cochecton in the last week of May and the subsequent departure of a number of prominent patriots, including Bezaleel Tyler, in the first days of June. By early June, 1778, Cochecton was thoroughly dominated by white and Indian Loyalists (see Hastings 3, p. 367-369, 375-376, 399-400, 505, 524, 541, 653; and 4, p. 271). The only Mohawks in Cochecton at that time were there to get provisions from the settlers, as the reports in the Clinton Papers make quite clear. They were not trying to scare the settlers away, as Nathan Skinner claims.

Another reason to discount the traditional account of raiding Mohawks is the presence of a Loyalist named Barnabus, Bernard, or Barney Kane, who was fighting with the Mohawks--Bryant is an Anglicization of the Dutch "Barent," which in English is Bernard or Barnabus ("Barney"). On November 3, 1778, Mohawk war captain Isaac Hill and Barney Kane took Peter Harper of Harpersfield prisoner (Draper 5F38). Barney Kane was serving under Joseph Brant in February, 1780, when he described the Whigs he had killed, placing a live baby at its dead mother's breast (see Priest, p. 18-19). Barnabus Kane is on the British Indian Service payroll as early as April 1779 as an Interpreter, and transferred to the corps of foresters by the summer of 1782 (Haldimand 21770:8, 21762:138-2). Barnabus Cain appears on the December 1, 1783, ration list at Niagara as aged 36 with a wife Margaret, aged 32, and son John, aged 9 (Haldimand 21765:375). The 1783 ration list probably means that Kane had remarried a widow, and her son John is called "John Cain" much as Moses Thomas II's children are ascribed to Asa Chapman (see note 34). (The ration list has some other gross errors: Robert Land, for example, is listed as age 30 in 1783.)

It seems extremely unlikely that Kane would fight alongside the very people--the Mohawks--who had slaughtered his family. The ferocious antagonism he later displayed to Whigs or Patriots would be explicable if a group of Whigs had actually killed his family, rather than a group of Mohawks.

Both Nathan Skinner and Quinlan (Pioneers, p. 148) say Mrs. Land and her eldest son John had taken their cattle into the woods to elude raiding Whig scouts at the time of the murders. The map shows that both the Kanes and the Lands were exposed to raiding parties from the south, the Kanes particularly so, since they lived the farthest south of any farm on the east side of the river, *the side which had the path from Minisink*. The party whom Nathan Skinner says followed after the raiding Mohawks-neighbors and Indians "friendly to liberty"--sounds quite like the group said to have burned the Land family's house in the Loyalist version of the story.

The question is, who were these raiders? In early July, 1778, Lt. Colonel John Butler of Butler's Rangers, poised to attack the forts at Wyoming, send a party of Rangers and Indians from Wyoming to the valley of the Lackawaxen to raid and take a few prisoners (Haldimand 21760:31, 21771:10). From two of the prisoners, Jaspar Parrish and James Pemberton, we learn that the Indians in this party were mostly Delawares and Tuscaroras (Parrish, p. 527-529). Joseph Brant, in the meantime, was at Onaquaga preparing a major raid down the Delaware, as Robert Jones reported to the Peenpack Committee of Safety:

> Brant then formed an expedition against Lakawak for the purpose of collecting provision and went one day on his march, when an express was sent after him requiring him to

return immediately, on account that a party
from the northward was expected to attack
Unadilla. Brant immediately returned [to
Onaquaga] . . . and last Sunday [July 5] said
Brant followed after [to Unadilla]. The same
day five Indians arrived at Aghquago [Ona-
quaga] and gave information of a large
number of Sinekes [Senecas] on their march
to the same place. . . . Examinent [Robert
Jones] at Anahquage . . . made his escape the
same day, who on his march says he met
about 20 Indians and white men with a
number of prisoners, which they told him
they had got at Lakawak. (Hastings 3, p. 543).

These 20 Indians and whites were the party sent out by
Butler, who had captured Jaspar Parrish; they passed
through Cochecton to Cookose (now Deposit). Parrish, who
wrote a complete account of his captivity, makes no mention
of any families murdered while he was a captive of the raiding party.

But this party of Indians and Rangers were not the only
ones passing through Cochecton at that time: the Peenpack
Committee of Safety reported to Governor Clinton on July 10
on the arrival "last evening . . . of Capt. Cuddeback from
Coshethton [Cochecton] where he had been with a small
scouting party" (Hastings 3, p. 541). The Peenpack Committee had been expecting an attack on Peenpack or Minisink
and had the militia ready, waiting for Joseph Brant and his
men to march down the Delaware. At Cushetunk, Captain
Cuddeback talked to Solomon Decker, who mistakenly
equated the Lakawaxen raiding party with Brant's men.
Solomon Decker also told Cuddeback that "there was still a
few lurking villains of the party at Lackawack," when in fact
these were a few of Brant's Mohawks and white volunteers
who had remained at Cochecton (Hastings 3, p. 542).

At the same time that the Peenpack Committee received
Robert Jones's intelligence telling them that most of Brant's
men were gone from both Cochecton and Onaquaga, the
people of Minisink witnessed "women and children by hun-
dreds . . . flocking from Wyoming where by the concurrent
testimony of numbers, the most horrid sceans [scenes] of

savage barbarity has been exhibited, and sundry families are moving from hence . . ." (Hastings 3, p. 540).

The Committee, "after we gained the intelligence by Capt. Cuddeback, thought best to dismiss the whole of our [militia] regiments except one class from each company" (ibid.). And so it happened that numbers of Patriot militia at Peenpack, with the horrors of Wyoming's refugees ringing in their ears, were released from military authority because Brant and most of his men were gone from both Cochecton and Onaquaga.

It's not impossible that one group of these dismissed militia, with some local Minisink Indians who were "friendly to liberty," went up the river path to the "nest of Tories" at Cochecton, encountered the Kane family, and revenged themselves for Wyoming. Such a group may have taken John Land prisoner (his first imprisonment, see note 58) and then followed the small "party of observation" Brant had left at Cochecton (one of whom probably warned Phoebe Land), and demanded Volunteer Abel Land as their prisoner. The Mohawks may then have tried to create the fiction that Abel was their own prisoner--making him run an unbelievably easy gauntlet--to protect him. As a Volunteer, Abel would have been put in prison, maybe hanged. As a prisoner of the Mohawks being returned, Abel might still keep his liberty. He did make his escape to New York, and John Land escaped to be recaptured scarcely six weeks later.

After the Revolution Bryant Kane returned to the Delaware Valley, living near Trenton, New Jersey, where he was known as a drunkard (Draper 17F172).

50. Local tradition has it that Mrs. Evans, being delayed, swam the Delaware carrying her child (Goodrich, p. 125). Nathaniel Evans was serving in the American army at the time, but Mrs. Evans was in Cochecton at the end of May, 1778 (Hastings, 3, p. 376). Nathan Skinner is mistaken on the number of persons in this group, since Mrs. Evans had at least three children by the end of 1776. It is possible that the story of the fleeing Mrs. Evans was confused with her flight in 1763. The Skinners and Smiths may have fled the Peenpack militia in April, 1777 (see note 48), returned to Cushetunk (see following note) and fled again at the time of the Kane family murders. This would explain Nathan Skinner's confu-

sion.

51. Daniel Skinner was still at Cochecton on June 2, 1778, when he signs a letter (with Benjamin Skinner, Joseph Ross, Nathan Mitchell, Gersham Smith, William Conklin, David Young, Lem'u Burchem, Solomon Decker, John Conklin, and Paulus) to Major John Decker, American militia, that there is no trouble at Cochecton saving the ruin of Moses Thomas' house, and they don't want the militia to come there (Hastings 3, p. 390). John Lassely is mentioned as a Whig (Patriot) in April, 1778 (Hastings 3, 193). He was married to Sarah Tyler, third daughter of Bezaleel Tyler I, and probably fled with Bezaleel II in June, 1778. Solomon Decker, although appearing as a Loyalist to his neighbors, is an informant to Captain [Abraham] Cuddeback in early July, 1778 (note 49 and Hastings 3, p. 542).

52. Col. Hooper appears nowhere in our searches. Skinner's statement, "as the office of the Governor then existed" refers to the fact that Pennsylvania was governed at that time by an executive council which supported Independence. It would seem that Joseph Ross was instrumental in influencing a good many of his neighbors to stay at Cochecton.

53. There is some doubt that this agreement was made, as is stated here, in 1777. Major John Decker of the Peenpack militia writes Governor George Clinton on June 8, 1778 (Hastings 3, p. 425-426) "a number of the inhabitants at Cusheton is torys and is gathering all the Endins [Indians] that the[y] can get to join them." Mrs. Wahl (p. 49) quotes a monument the State of Pennsylvania erected at Milanville, Pennsylvania [Cushetunk]: "Settlement seized by the Indians and Tories, 1778." This obviously refers to the above-mentioned agreement. If this agreement was actually made, as Nathan Skinner states, immediately after the murder of Bryant Kane's family, then the murder would have actually taken place in late June or early July 1778 (see note 49).

54. Bezaleel Tyler II. The real name of "Captain Mush" was omitted from Arthur N. Meyers edition of *The Nathan Skinner Manuscript.*

74

55. The probability that Bezaleel Tyler was captain of the Second, or South End regiment of the Ulster County militia is discussed in Leslie, p. 182-183.

56. The name Monoto must refer to a local Delaware Indian leader, since the name appears as early as 1 June, 1660, when Indians living near the Menissing [Minisink] Indians "fled in fear of a certain Maniito" (O'Callighan and Fernow 12, p. 315). Jaspar Parrish reported eight Delaware families living at Cookhose (Deposit, N.Y.) in July, 1778, but said their leader was a Captain Mounsh (Parrish, p. 528).

57. Local tradition says that Nathan Mitchell, a native of Litchfield, Connecticut, remained at Cochecton because his wife refused to leave her father, Joseph Ross (Matthews, p. 452, 456). However, B. T. Mitchell, a grandson of Nathan Mitchell, wrote Lyman Draper that his grandmother fled to Bound Brook, New Jersey, aftering hearing of the Kane family murders. She departed without warning her husband, who was upriver at the time. B. T. Mitchell also wrote that the Kanes were murdered by the Mohawks by mistake, their intended targets being the Mitchells and John and Elias Conklin (Draper 17F175e). B. T. Mitchell was trying to convince Draper that his grandfather was a Patriot, however. The Mitchells were Loyalists, and Mrs. Mitchell, as a daughter of Joseph Ross, was under Brant's and the Mohawks' "special protection" (see note 27). The idea that the Mitchells were threatened by the Mohawks is thus absurd. If Mrs. Mitchell did flee, she was fleeing a Patriot scouting or raiding party. The Conklins-Nicholas Conklin and his sons John and Elias--were Patriots, but they lived two miles upriver of the Kanes, with the Mitchells between. They may have already fled to Minisink by the time of the murder (Hastings 3, p. 367-368). Given the Kane family's distinctive location opposite Cochecton Falls, the probability of "mistake" is highly unlikely. Moreover, there is no authentic record that Joseph Brant (who commanded at Onaquaga) or Mohawks under him killed any women and children at any time in the Revolution.

58. John Land, born probably in 1758, was the oldest son of Robert and Phoebe (Scott) Land (Wahl, p. 57). According to

Quinlan (Pioneers, p. 159), John Land was arrested and thrown into the Log Jail in New Jersey once, escaped for a brief time, and was retaken and reinterred in the Log Jail. The story of his recapture resembles Nathan Skinner's version of the capture of John Land. Quinlan goes on to say that Land was released in the custody of a man named Joel Harvey, for whom he worked until the end of the war. Land then returned to Cochecton and purchased his father's old land. He married Lillie Skinner, daughter of Daniel Skinner (Wahl, p. 53), and built the oldest house still standing in Milanville, in 1796.

There is some doubt, however, that this house is on the site of the original Robert Land house. The John Land "Red House" is north of Calkin's Creek (Nat. Park Service and our map). It was purchased by Nathan Skinner in 1814 (*The Wayne Independent*). In 1815, Skinner built another house, south of Calkin's Creek near the river in present day Milanville, and later gave this house to his son, Col. Calvin Skinner (see note 45 and Beers, p. 28). Robert Land had "settled on the property now owned by Colonel Calvin Skinner, at Milanville, and it was from that home that Mrs. Land went . . ." (Matthews, p. 457). Evidently this property had been owned first by Aaron Thomas (Skinner manuscript, p. 5 and note 13) who later, probably after the 1763 raid, moved near John Lassely (Matthews, p. 457). Such a location, near the river just south of Calkin's Creek, would make sense in terms of Phoebe Land's attempted rescue of the Kanes, and it would have been particularly exposed to raiders from the south during the Revolution.

59. Bezaleel Tyler also left an account of this raid, very different in tone from Nathan Skinner's (Hastings 3, p. 634-635):

> Peenpack August the 14 1778 "Dear Coll. This morning Mr. Tylar came to see me after his return from Coschecton [Cochecton] last night and brings the following acc't.
> Last Monday in the afternoon Mr. Tylar set out from Lieut. Decker's with 37 men in order to go up to Coschecton [Cochecton] and on their march at the mouth of the Lagawack

[Lackawack], they met with a company of the standing forces which came from Coll. Stroud's, and a part of the Pennsylvania and Jersey militia, which in the whole amounted to 230 men, and so marched up to Cochecton. And Mr. Tylar was on the advance guard with his party and took one Barkar prisoner, and examined him strickly, who said that there was no enemy near. But Mr. Tylar still advanced about two miles and he, being on the flank guard, espied a party of Indians coming down. Upon which he and his men squatted and let them pass to the main body, and then went down and lay in ambush with an intent to cut off their retreat, but they were soon discovered by a party that was in the rear, who fired on them. Upon which they retreated, but discovering a party on the mountain they took to the river, and the men in ambush fired on them and made some of them fall.

They took two prisoners more who said that the party which was a coming down were intended for Minisink. Likewise the two prisoners, told Mr. Tylar that there was thirty Indians and five white men in the party they met, and another party a coming down of a hundred. But one of the prisoners told the commander of the standing forces that Butler was a coming down with his army, upon which he ordered his men to march back. And after they marched, Capt'n Van Atten of Pennsylvania and Capt'n Tylar with a few men advanced a mile further and killed an Indian and brought off from the enemy some plunder. In the whole they took three white men prisoners and killed one. Likewise [they] killed and wounded four Indians. From your friend & Hum'le Ser't

Jacob Newkerk.

To Coll. John Cantine [of Marbletown]

Tyler says he took three white men prisoners, and Nathan

Skinner likewise credits him with three, but the lists do not agree, for if Tyler took "one Barker" prisoner as well as Mitchell, Davis, and John Land, he would have had four. Tyler says he also killed a white--possibly Cooley (see note 42).

Other raids occurred, most notably in the week before November 15, 1778, by the Peenpack militia (Hastings 4, p. 276). This may have been precipitated by the October 13, 1778, raid of Joseph Brant on Peenpack. There was an American troop buildup in the Minisink area starting in November, 1779 (Leslie, p. 8-17). Both infantry and cavalry under Count Pulaski were sent to the vicinity of Cole's Fort (the cavalry was later withdrawn), followed by orders to General Hand from General Washington to take command of the troops in the area:

> I have thought it would be more agreeable to you to move down to the Minisink settlement and take the command of a Body of troops which we are under the necessity of assembling there to protect that frontier against the incursions of the Indians. The Corps at the Minisink will consist of Count Pulaski's Legion, Colo. Armand's Corps and Colo. Spencer's Regt. making about 500 Horse and Foot. Colo. Cortlands Regt. is at Rochester in the neighborhood of Minisink. (Fitzpatrick 13, p. 293).

This raid and the ensuing troop buildup must have alarmed the Loyalist inhabitants of the Upper Delaware, for a letter, signed by four Indian chiefs under Joseph Brant, was sent to Colonel John Cantine, commander of the local militia:

> Decemb'r 13th 1778
> Joseph Brant
> Mr. Capt: Sir, It is the desire of the Seneca chiefs and other Indians that you will not in the least trouble or molest those people on the Delaware above Econack [Equinunk] . . . It is, therefore, the desire of us Indians that those people living about Shackaken [Shehawken] are our brothers; we, therefore, desire that

you will let our brothers live in peace, lest you
be worst dealt with, than your neighbours the
Cherry Valley People was . . . But if you de-
stroy that place, I will set my face again you,
for if you hurt my people I shall fell the
stroke, for the Six Nations fells the stroke that
hurts their brothers.
Capt. William Johnson, Chief Mohack
[Mohawk]; Joseph Ceskwrora [Tuscarora],
Chief; Capt. John, Chief; William George,
Chief. (Hastings 3, p. 364)

Captain William Johnson, Tegawirunte, was the half-
Mohawk son of Sir William Johnson and one of the few
Mohawks who could read and write in English. A Joseph
Kanondagerha is listed under the Onaquagans and Tuscaro-
ras claiming losses after the Revolution ("Memorandum of the
different Sums and Claims . . . left behind in 1777. . . .", Q
Series, vol. 24, part 2, p. 322, National Archives of Canada).
Captain John is described in note 39, and William George,
possibly the son of Delaware George, is mentioned in a story
about Tom Quick (Quinlan, Sullivan County, p. 372), who
encountered William George on the Pennsylvania side of the
Delaware at Pond Eddy sometime before the war.

60. Although Skinner places Russ' Brook and Abram's
swamp on the Jersey (New York) side, the only stream that
enters the river "a little above this [Big] Island" does not lead
to either a swamp or a valley. The stream that enters from
the east about midway down Big Island is where, by most
local sources, William Conklin first lived. It drains to Tama-
rack Swamp, which also drains to East Callicoon Creek. The
stream on the west side of the river far better fits Skinner's
description of Russ' Brook (U.S. Geological Survey; our map),
and agrees with his story that Russ was living on that side of
the river in 1767, when Mrs. Russ, her sister, and Mrs. Clark
fought Daniel Skinner's wife.

61. The story of the killing of Abraham Russ and his son
Cyrus is given in Quinlan's Pioneers (p. 213-223). Abraham
Russ and --- Van Etten had married two sisters, and Van
Etten and his family had migrated to the Ohio River after the

Revolution. Russ and his family followed, with a grown son, Cyrus Russ. A grown daughter who had married Benjamin Jones of Shehawken stayed on the Delaware. Russ and Van Etten's mother-in-law, Russ himself, Cyrus Russ, and a baby were murdered by a band of hostile Indians, who had come to the Van Etten cabin. Mrs. Russ, Mr. and Mrs. Van Etten, and various younger children escaped. Mrs. Russ returned to the Delaware and married a man named George Hawk.

Abraham Russ was married to Huldah Thomas in 1767 (see Nathan Skinner's text), but she may not have been the mother of Cyrus or his grown sister; her mother died in 1779 (note 26). Huldah Thomas was probably Russ's second wife, and the slaughtered mother-in-law the mother of his first wife and of Mrs. Van Etten, since Nathan Skinner seems to imply that Huldah Thomas Russ was not killed at the time of this massacre.

REFERENCES

Anderson, Marjorie Thomas, 1990, *The Thomas Saga on the Upper Delaware and the Norton Connection*, privately published, Indian Lake, NY.

Boyd, Julian, 1962-1964, *The Susquehannah Company Papers*, volume 1: 1750-1755, volume 2: 1756-1767, Wyoming Historical & Geological Society and Cornell University Press, Ithaca, NY.

Beauchamp, William, 1912, *Aboriginal Place Names of New York*. New York State Museum Bulletin 108, New York State Education Department, Albany.

Beers, F. W., editor, 1872, map of Damascus Township and towns therein, *Atlas of Wayne County, Pennsylvania*, A. Pomeroy & Co., New York, p. 28-30.

Campbell, Marjorie Freeman, 1966, *A Mountain and a City: The Story of Hamilton*, McClelland & Stewart, Ltd., Toronto/Montreal.

Chapman, Isaac A., 1830, *A Sketch of the History of Wyoming by the Late Isaac A. Chapman, Esq. to Which is Added an Appendix Containing a Statistical Account of the Valley, and Adjacent Country*, Sharp D. Lewis, Wilkes-Barre, PA.

Clearwater, A. T., 1907, *History of Ulster County, New York*, W. J. Van Deusen, New York, NY.

Coleman, Charles C., compiler, 1934, *Early Records of the First Presbyterian Church at Goshen, New York*, privately published.

Coleman, John M., 1956, "Robert Land and Some Frontier Skirmishes," *Ontario History*, v. 48, no. 2, p. 47-62.

Cottle, Elizabeth S., 1989, "Nathaniel Evans: A Frontier Soldier," *Tallow Light* (a publication of the Washington County, Ohio, Historical Society), v. 20, no. 2, p. 67-72.

Cruikshank, Ernest Alexander, 1893, *The Story of Butler's Rangers and the Settlement of Niagara*, Lundy's Lane Historical Society, Welland, Ontario.

Day, Richard E., compiler, 1909, *Calendar of the Sir William Johnson Manuscripts in the New York State Library*, State of New York, Albany.

de Peyster, John Watts, 1888, "A New and Accurate Map of the Provinces of Pennsylvania, Virginia, Maryland, and New Jersey" [originally published in 1762], *Appendix, Explanatory Notes, &ct., &ct., &ct.*, A. F. Chasmar & Co., New York (map follows Addenda at end of Volume).

Dorrance, Francis, editor, 1923, "Westmoreland Probate Records," *Wyoming Historical & Geological Society*, v. 18, Wilkes-Barre, PA.

Draper, Lyman Copeland, n.d., Joseph Brant Papers, F series, 15 volumes, Historical Society of Wisconsin, Madison, WI.

Egle, William H., editor, 1893, "Documents Relating to the Connecticut Settlement of the Wyoming Valley," *Pennsylvania Archives, 2nd Series*, v. 18, pts. 1 and 2.

Fitzpatrick, John C., editor, 1931-1944, *The Writings of George Washington from Original Manuscript Sources, 1745-1799*, 39 volumes, U.S. Government Printing Office, Washington, DC.

Fonda, Jelles, 1755-1775, "Account Book, Probably Jelles Fonda's" (on microfilm at the Cornell University library, Ithaca, NY).

Fryer, Mary Beacock, and Lt. Col. William A. Smy, 1981, *Rolls of the Provincial (Loyalist) Corps, Canadian Command, American Revolutionary Period*, Dundurn Canadian Historical Document Series Publication #1, Toronto, Ontario.

Goodrich, Phineas G., 1888, *History of Wayne County*, Haynes and Beardsley, Nonesdale, PA.

Gray, Elma E., 1956, Wilderness Christians: *The Moravian Mission to the Delaware Indians*, Cornell University Press, Ithaca, NY.

Green, Ernest, 1911, "Some Graves on Lundy's Lane," *Niagara Historical Society Publication #22*, 73 pp.

Haldimand, Sir Frederick, 1772-1787, Unpublished papers, British Museum Additional MSS, 232 volumes (on microfilm at the Newberry Library, Chicago, Illinois).

Hamilton, Milton, 1979, *Sir William Johnson, Colonial American*, National University Publications and Kennekat Press, New York, NY.

Hastings, Hugh, editor, 1899-1900, *The Public Papers of George Clinton, War of the Revolution Series*, volumes 2 (1899), 3 and 4 (1900), State of New York, Albany.

Harvey, Oscar Jewell, 1909-1927, *A History of Wilkes-Barre*, 4 volumes, Wilkes-Barre, Pennsylvania (volumes 3 and 4 completed by Ernest Gray Smith).

Hazard, Samuel, 1852-1856, *Pennsylvania Archives, 1st Series*, volumes 2 (1852) and 4 (1853), Joseph Severns & Co., Philadelphia.

Holland Society, 1906, "Records of the Reformed Dutch Church of Albany," *Year Book of the Holland Society for 1906*, p. 1-179.

Hopkins, Timothy, 1903, *The Kelloggs in the Old World and the New*, volume 1, Sunset Press and Photo Engraving Co., San Francisco, CA.

Kelsay, Isabel, 1984, *Joseph Brant 1743-1807 Man of Two Worlds*, Syracuse University Press, Syracuse, NY.

Land, John H., 1901, "Story of Robert Land, U.E. Loyalist," *Niagara Historical Society Publication #8* (reprinted 1919), p. 39-43.

Leslie, Vernon, 1975, *The Battle of Minisink*, T. Emmett Henderson, Publisher, Middletown, NY.

Matthews, Albert, 1886, *History of Wayne, Pike and Monroe Counties, Pennsylvania*, R. T. Peck and Co., Philadelphia, PA.

Meyers, Arthur N., 1970, *The Nathan Skinner Manuscript*, Delaware Valley Press, Narrowsburg, NY.

Miner, Charles, 1845, *History of Wyoming in a Series of Letters*, J. Crissy Publisher, Philadelphia.

Minutes of the Provincial Council of Pennsylvania, from the Organization to the Termination of the Proprietary Government, volumes 5, 6 and 8, 1851, Theo. Fenn & Company, Harrisburg (referred to in the notes as *Pa. Col. Rec.*).

National Archives of Canada, *Records Relating to Indian Affairs*, RG 10, A2, volumes 1824, 1827, and 1828.

National Park Service, 1982, *Cultural Resource Survey*, Volume 1, Summary and Recommendations, p. 1-78-1-79 and Volume 5, Historical Architecture.

Nelson, Paul David, 1990, *William Tryon and the Course of Empire*, University of North Carolina Press, Chapel Hill, NC.

Nelson, William, editor, 1906, *Documents Relating to the Revolutionary History of the State of New Jersey (2nd Series)*, volume 3, John L. Murphy Publishing Co., Trenton, NJ.

New York Genealogical and Biographical Society, 1937, "Records of Trinity Church Parrish, New York City," *New York Genealogical and Biographical Record*, v. 65, p. 379.

New York Historical Society, 1916, "Proceedings of a Board of General Officers of the British Army at New York, *Collections*, p. 152.

O'Callaghan, E. B., and B. Fernow, editors, 1853-1887, *Documents Relative to the Colonial History of New York*, 15 volumes, State of New York, Albany.

Ontario, Bureau of Archives, 1905, *Third Report for 1904.*

Ontario Historical Society, 1919, "Petition of Abel Land," *Ontario Historical Society Papers and Records*, v. 24, p. 84.

Palmer, Gregory, 1984, *Biographical Sketches of Loyalists of the American Revolution*, Meckler Publications, Westport, CT.

Parrish, Stephen, compiler, 1903, "The Story of Jasper Parrish," *Buffalo Historical Society Publications*, v. 6, p. 527-546.

Powell, William S., 1980-1981, *The Correspondence of William Tryon and Other Selected Papers*, 2 volumes, North Carolina Division of Archives and History, Raleigh, NC.

Priest, Josiah, 1833, *Captivity and Suffering of Gen. of Freegift Patchin of Blenheim*, Packard, Hoffman, and White, Albany, NY (reprinted by Garland Publishing Co. *Indian Captivities*, vol. 52, 1977), p. 13-24.

Quick, Arthur C., 1942, *A Genealogy of the Quick Family*, privately published in South Haven and Palisades Park, Michigan.

Quinlan, James Eldridge, 1851, *Tom Quick The Indian Slayer and the Pioneers of Minisink and Wawarsink*, DeVoe and Quinlan, Publishers, Monticello, NY.

Quinlan, James Eldridge, 1873, *History of Sullivan County*, W. T. Morgans & Co., Liberty, NY.

Quinlan, James Eldridge, 1894, *The Original Life and Adventures of Tom Quick, The Indian Slayer*, "The Deposit Journal," Deposit, NY.

Scott, Kenneth, abstracter, 1972, *Genealogical Data from Administration Papers from the New York State Court of Appeals in Albany*, The National Society of Colonial Dames in the State of New York, New York, NY.

Smith, Phillip H., 1887, *Legends of the Shawangunk*, Smith & Co., Pawling, NY (reprinted in 1965 by Syracuse University Press, Syracuse, NY).

Smith, William, 1971, *Historical Memoirs from 26 Aug 1778 to 12 Nov 1783* (edited by William H. W. Sabine), Arno Press, New York, NY.

Snell, James P., compiler, 1881, *History of Sussex and Warren Counties, New Jersey*, volume 1, Everts & Peck, Philadelphia.

Sprenger, Bernice Cox, 1981, *Guide to the Manuscripts in the Burton Historical Collection*, Detroit Public Library, Detroit.

Stover, Shiela, 1982, *Ancestors and Descendants of Timothy Kellam*, available at the Equinunk Historical Society, Equinunk, PA.

The Sullivan Clinton Campaign in 1779, 1929, University of the State of New York, Albany.

Sullivan, James, Alexander C. Flick, and Milton W. Hamilton, editors, 1929 - 1965, *The Sir William Johnson Papers*, 14 volumes, State University of New York Press, Albany.

Taylor, Robert J., editor, 1968, *The Susquehannah Company Papers*, volume 6, 1774-1775, Wyoming Historical & Geological Society and Cornell University Press, Ithaca, NY.

Trowbridge, Francis Bacon, 1896, *Ashley Genealogy*, privately published, New Haven, CT.

U.S. Geological Survey, 1968 (revised 1980), 7.5 Minute Series Topographic Maps of the Damascus and Callicoon Quadrangles, New York and Pennsylvania (scale: 1:24,000).

Vosburgh, Royden Woodward, ed., 1917, "Records of the High and Low Dutch Reformed Congregation at Schoharie," volume 1, part 1, New York Genealogical and Biographical Society (on microfilm at the Newberry Library, Chicago, Illinois).

Wahl, Doris Seymour (Mrs. Gordon A.), compiler, 1957, *The Skinner Kinsmen: The Descendants of Joseph and Martha (Kinne) Skinner of Connecticut, New York, and Pennsylvania*, Niagara Falls, NY.

Wallace, Anthony C., 1949, *Teedyuscung, King of the Delawares*, University of Pennsylvania Press, Philadelphia.

Wallace, Paul A. W., 1945, *Conrad Weiser, 1696-1760: Friend of Colonist and Mohawk*, University of Pennsylvania Press, Philadelphia and London.

Wallace, Paul A. W., 1987, *Indian Paths of Pennsylvania*, Pennsylvania Historical and Museum Commission, Harrisburg.

The Waynesville Independent, 1969, "The Oldest House," November 20, 1969 (reprinted in Damascus Manor, by Alsup Vail Tyler, p. 59-63).

Weslager, Clinton A., 1972, *The Delaware Indians*, Rutgers University Press, New Brunswick, New Jersey.

INDEX

---, Aunt Hannah 15 Aunt
   Huldah 29 Aunt Nab 29
   Cyrus 29 Uncle Russ 29
ABEL, 68
ABLE, 69
ADAMS, 6 48 Deliverance 6
   48 49 Elizabeth 6 James
   4 5 8 35 45 48 49 Jona-
   than 49 Lydia 49 Sarah
   48 Wife of Deliverance 49
   William 49
ALLAN, 54 69
ALLEN, 10 55 Ebenezer 54
   Lucy 10 Wm 4
AMHERST, Jeffrey 44 Sir
   Jeffrey 45
APPLEMAN, Elizabeth 11
ARMAND, Colo 78
ASHLEY, 8 35 52 Mrs Moses
   Thomas 8 Benj 2 Benja-
   min 35-37 52 David 36
   Jonathan 36 Mrs 37
   Rebecca 36 Robert 36
   Sarah 52 Susannah 36
BALDWIN, Jeduthan 56
BANCROFT, Susannah 36
BARENT, 70
BARKAR, 77
BARKER, 78
BARNES, Abram 56 Rebecca
   12 Ruth 56 Thomas 12

BARNS, John 2
BEAMER, John 11 Katy 11
BEAUCHAMP, William 31
BLUNT, Ambrose 39
BOLTON, Mason 61
BRADDOCK, Edward 41
BRANDT, Captain 69 Joseph
   69
BRANT, 53 56 66 72 73 75
   Joseph 52 54 61 62 66
   70-72 78
BRINK, Hester 12
BROWN, Eben 49
BRYANT, 70
BUCK, Mary 40
BURCHAM, Lemuel 8 9
   Sarah 10
BURCHARD, John 34
BURCHEM, Lem'u 74
BURCHIM, Lemuel 8
BUSH, Abigail 27 Eli 11 28
   George 2 13 28 Hank 59
   Hannah 11 Hesiah 27
   John 28 Nelly 28 Polly 27
   Simeon 10 11 27 28
   Weighty 27
BUTLER, 72 John 71 Zebu-
   lon 56
CADOSHE, 8 9 58
CAIN, Barnabus 71 Brian 69
   John 71 Margaret 71

89

CALKIN, 55 Abigail 11 55
Bezaleel 28 Dr 11 55 Dr
John 45 Elam 55 Hannah
56 Hannah Thomas 64
John 10 26 35 55 John O
11 John Oliver 55 Moses
28 55 Nellie 28 Oliver 28
54-56 64 Phoebe 55
Sarah 28 55 64 Simeon 3
5 35 45 49 55 Sim[e]on 4
Weighty 28
CAMPBELL, 65
CANN, John 65
CANTINE, John 77 78
CARLSON, R 13
CARTRIGHT, David 67
CASH, 8 Daniel 43
CAYENQUEREGO, Jno 60
CHAMBERS, 53 54 Jacobus
53
CHAPMAN, 57 58 Abigail 57
58 Asa 56 57 71 Isaac A
34 Lucy 10 Nathan 10 35
43 Polly 10 Sarah 56
CLARK, 13 Mrs 14 15 16 79
Nathan 39 Phineas 13 14
20
CLAUS, Daniel 33 62
CLINTON, George 74 Gover-
nor 66 72 Sir Henry 65
COIT, --- 65
COMFORT, Elizabeth 11
CONKLIN, 9 54 68 Abigail 27
Benjamin 28 Betsy 28
Elias 27 28 75 Elizabeth
19 27 28 Hannah 28
Hester 27 Jacob 28 John
26-28 75 Joseph 28 Land
28 Nicholas 12 17 19 20
22 27-29 64 68 75 Paul
27 Rachel 12 27 28
Samuel 28 Sarah 28

CONKLIN (continued)
Steen 27 Stene 28 William
9 19 27 28 54 74 79
Yonne 28
COOLEY, 18 62 78 Reuben
20 62
CORBIN, Thomas 5
CORKINS, John 35 Simon 35
CORTLAND, Colo 78
COVEY, Barbara L 60
CROGHAN, George 62 Mr 41
CUDDEBACK, 72 Capt 72 73
Capt'n 66 Captain
(Abraham) 74
CUMMINS, 43
CURTIS, James C 52 John
34 Mary 58
D'WITT, J R 65
DAVIS, 25 26 78
DECKER, Ceort 20 John 74
Lieut 76 Reuben 56 Sarah
56 Solomon 24 72
Yohannes 20
DECRAIN, Mortimas 20
DENNY, Jacob 50
DEPUI, Aaron 34
DEPUY, Benjamin 20 22 65
DEWITT, Garton 59
DICKINSON, Sarah 36
DRAKE, Abigail 12 Charles
12 28 Christina 12 Jesse
12 28 John 9 10 Martha
12 Mr 67 Mrs Jesse 28
Patty 28 Teeney 28
DRAPER, Lyman 75
DREMOR, 8
DREMORE, 8
DUSINBURG, John 48
EDWARD, Hannah 12 Wil-
liam 12
EDWARDS, Jonathan 37
ELIOT, Jemima 32 John 32

90

MITCHELL (continued)
Jinnie 28 John 28 Joseph
11 28 Lydia 28 Mrs 75
Nathan 25 28 29 68 70 74
75 Polly 28 Sarah 28
Stephen 28
MITCHELLS, 23 (family) 68
75
MOORE, John 34
MORDON, 67 Ralph 67
MUSH, Captain 24 25 27 74
NATHAN, Skinner 62
NELSON, Paul David 65
NEWKERK, Capt'n 66 Jacob
77
OLIVER, Mr 37
OWEN, Enoch 11 Lois 11 Mr
11
PARK, Nathan 44
PARKS, 59 Benjamin 34
David 11 Josiah 13 29 58
59 Moses 59 Nathan 8 43
59 Sarah 11 William 59
PARRISH, 72 Jaspar 71 72
75
PATTERSON, Nemiah 20
PAULUS, 74
PAYNE, Dr 35
PEABODY, 34
PEMBERTON, James 71
PENN, Lord 42 Richard 63
64 William 60
PENNIN, James 43
PEPPERRELL, William 41
PETERS, Hendrick 33
PHINEAS, Clark 20
PHOEBE, 68
PITKIN, Lt 37
POWELL, Brig Gen 67
PRESTON, Judge 53
PRICE, Wm 2
PULASKI, Count 78

QUENAMECKQUID, Charles
60
QUICK, 53 54 Harriet 12
Thomas Sr 47 Tom 5 29
47 48 53 79 Tom Jr 48
Tom Junior 47
QUINLAN, 31 38 39 49 50 62
68 71 75 James Eldridge
48
RIBLE, Abigail 11 James 11
RICHARDSON, 4 Lille 4
Phoebe 4 21
ROSS, 52 53 Hinne 27 Isaac
27 James 11 27 John 12
27 Joseph 8 9 19 24 27
29 52 64 69 74 75 Peggy
12 27 Rachel 27 Sarah 11
Sophia 12
RUSS, 8 9 13 79 80 Abra-
ham 13 14 79 80 Cyrus
79 80 Huldah 14 15 16
80 Huldah Thomas 80
Mrs 79 80
SALISBURY, Esther 11 Mr
11
SARAH, Aunt 10
SCOTT, 66 Gelosha 11
General 11 Phoebe 65 75
Winfield 66
SHEPHERD, Katy 11
SHIMER, Abraham 48
SKINNER, 5 13-15 20 21 38
55 60 64 70 74 76 79
Abner 3 35 Abraham 20
Admiral 29 Benjamin 3-5
35 38 52 74 Calvin 3 6 50
64 66 76 Colonel Calvin
50 Conrad 38 Courtland
27 Dan'l 69 Daniel 2-5 7
8 12-14 17-21 23 24 27
34 35 39 50 52 58 64 67
74 79 Daniel Jr 50

93

SKINNER (continued)
Danl 40 Ebenezer 7
Gideon 35 Haggai 3 13
17-19 38 64 69 Huldah 3
Jeptha 7 John 3 Joseph 2
3 4 8 10 35 37 41 50 Lillie
14 27 28 76 Martha 3
Mary 27 Millicent 52 Mr
37 Mrs 14 16 17 Nathan
27 31 34 40 43 45-48 54-
58 64 70 71 73 74 76 77
80 Phoebe 14-16 50
Reuben 14 27 Sarah 27
Sarah Calkin 64 Timothy
3-5 34 35 38 William 27
38
SKINNERS, 7 8 (family) 73
SMITH, 21 Charles 56 70
George 12 Gersham 74
Gershom 21 23 24
Hannah 11 John 4 5 35
Phoebe 21 23
SMITHS, (family) 73
SPAULDING, Simeon 61
SPENCER, Colo 78
STANTON, 34
STENTON, John 45
STONE, William L 60
STREET, 11
STROBO, 62 Captain 61
STROUD, Coll 77
SWARTOUT, Philip 22
SWARTWOUT, 65 Philip 65
THOMAS, 7 42 50 56 (Mrs)
Moses 8 Aaron 5 6 8 19
35 43 45 56 64 76 Abigail
12 56 Benjamin 6 Capt 58
Charity 6 Cyrus 6 Dolly 6
Elias 6 50 56 Elsie 6
Hannah 6 12 28 56
Huldah 6 80 James 6
Joseph 6 11 26 57 58

THOMAS (continued)
Judge 49 52 Lois 6 Molly
6 Moses 5 12 14 15 26 28
34 35 42 43 45 56 74
Moses I 6 8 45 49 52
Moses II 6 12 55-58 71
Moses III 28 49 56 Mrs 28
Phoebe 11 Rachel 6 Ruth
12 28 56 Sarah 6 12 28
52 56 Uncle Moses 14
TRACEY, Christopher 43
Elisha 34 Isaac 34 43
Jonathan 43
TRIM, 34
TRYON, 65 Mr 22 William 64
TURKEY, 8
TYLAR, Capt'n 77 Mr 76 77
TYLER, 25 43 54 55 77 78
Abigail 10-12 27 28 55 56
Able 11 12 Abner 20
Amos 10 12 27 Benjamin
28 Bezaleel 11 21 24 28
56 70 74 76 Bezaleel I 6 8
10-12 27 55 56 74 Beza-
leel II 10 11 27 45 54 55
74 Bezaleel II (wife of) 10
Bill 12 Captain 25 26 62
70 Catherine 27 Charles
10 11 27 David 12 Ebe-
nezer 27 Elam 11 27 55
Elizabeth 11 12 27
Ephraim 58 Esabel 12
Gelosha 11 George 27
Hannah 10 11 12 Harriet
12 Hester 12 Isabel 12
John 11 12 27 28 55
Joseph 58 Katy 11 Lillie
11 12 Lina 12 Lois 11
Lydia 28 Martha 12 Mary
56 Molly 10 12 Moses 11
13 27 28 55 Nathaniel 10
11 Olida 12

TYLER (continued)
Oliver 11 27 28 55 Paul
10 12 27 Peggy 12 Phoebe
11 12 27 55 Polly 11 12
27 Rachel 11 12 Rebecca
10 12 27 Rockram 12
Sarah 10-12 27 55 74
Silas 10-12 Sophia 10 12
27 Thomas 12 Timothy 10
12 20 27 William 10 12
27 56 Wm 26 Yenachee
11 Yeneachy 11 Yenechy
28
TYLER, 26
TYLER THOMAS, Sarah 57
VAIL, Mary 56
VAN---, Elizabeth 12 Moses
12
VANATTEN, Capt'n 77
VANAUKEN, Abraham 18 19
20
VANCE, Yenachee 11
Yeneachy 11 Yenechy 28
VANCY, Yenachee 11
Yeneachy 11
VANETTEN, 79 80 Mr 80
Mrs 80
VANEVERAN, Dav'd 59
VANFROEGOR, Hamanut 22
VANINWEGEN, Jerardus 65
VANYLE, Isaac 20

WAHL, Mrs 74
WAINRIGHT, John 12 Lillie
12
WALLACE, Anthony F C 38
WALTON, Henry 39
WASHINGTON, General 78
George 41 67
WEISER, Conrad 32 61 62
Mr 32
WELSH, James 18 62
WENTS, Timothy 39
WESTBROOK, Anthony 20
Lanas 20 Leneus 20
WILLIAMSON, 44 John 43
WILLING, Thomas 5
WILLIS, 7 49 50 Jeddediah 4
5 Jedediah 35 Jedediah
Jr 35
WINTS, Timothy 3
WISNER, Henry 20
WITTER, 7 Ezra 5
WITTERS, 50 51
WOOD, John 62 Jonas 69
WOODBRIDGE, Jemima 32
John 32 Timothy 31 32
WYLLY, Samuel 49
YAQUEEKHON, Nicholas 60
YOUNG, 54 David 9 27 29 52
54 74 Elizabeth 9 Esabel
12 George 27 Isabel 12 27
John 27 Thomas 27

www.ingramcontent.com/pod-product-compliance
Lightning Source LLC
Chambersburg PA
CBHW071058090426
42737CB00013B/2374